Tackling Wicked Government Problems

INNOVATIONS IN LEADERSHIP

The Innovations in Leadership series, a collaboration of the Olin Business School at Washington University in St. Louis and the Brookings Institution Press, offers books that are succinct, action-oriented, and pragmatic, focused on a wide range of problems facing business and government leaders today. Each title will offer practical approaches and innovative solutions to meet present-day challenges.

Washington University and the Brookings Institution share the indelible stamp of philanthropist and businessman Robert S. Brookings, an innovator in responsible private enterprise and effective governance, who founded the Brookings Institution and was a major benefactor of the university and chairman of its board of trustees. The series seeks to emulate Brookings's legacy in seeking and informing in order to achieve a balance in the public and private sectors leading to improved governance at all levels of American public and private life.

Also in this series:

Leading Change in a Web 2.1 World: How Changecasting Builds Trust, Creates Understanding, and Accelerates Organizational Change
Jackson Nickerson

Tackling Wicked Government Problems

A Practical Guide for Developing Enterprise Leaders

JACKSON NICKERSON
RONALD SANDERS
editors

BROOKINGS INSTITUTION PRESS
Washington, D.C.

Copyright © 2013

THE BROOKINGS INSTITUTION
1775 Massachusetts Avenue, N.W., Washington, D.C. 20036
www.brookings.edu

Library of Congress Cataloging-in-Publication data
Tackling wicked government problems : a practical guide for developing enterprise leaders / Jackson Nickerson and Ronald Sanders, editors.
    pages cm. — (Innovations in leadership)
Includes bibliographical references and index.
ISBN 978-0-8157-2507-7 (hardcover : alk. paper)
1. Government executives—United States. 2. Administrative agencies—United States—Management. 3. Executive departments—United States—Management. 4. Interagency coordination—United States. 5. Organizational effectiveness—United States. 6. Leadership—United States. I. Nickerson, Jackson A. II. Sanders, Ronald P., 1951–
JK723.E9T33 2013
352.30973--dc23   2013020601

9 8 7 6 5 4 3 2 1

Printed on acid-free paper

Typeset in Sabon and Ocean

Composition by Oakland Street Publishing
Arlington, Virginia

Printed by R. R. Donnelley
Harrisonburg, Virginia

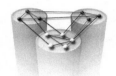

Contents

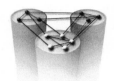# Preface

The federal government has a leadership crisis. The problem does not originate from its career executives or those that aspire to be. Without exception or doubt, career executives are unequivocally committed to their country and to the ideals of its public service, as well as to the missions of the agencies they serve. Nor does the problem come strictly from agencies, which, to varying degrees, have invested in developing their own leaders, readying them for the difficult agency challenges they face.

No, the leadership crisis derives from an institutional failure. As an institution, the federal government has no systematic, "whole-of-government" approach for developing its career executives. The original vision of the Senior Executive Service cast career executives as a government-wide, *enterprise* leadership corps with the understanding and ability to tackle wicked challenges that span multiple government agencies. However, in the years since the 1979 inception of the Senior Executive Service, executive development has remained decidedly agency-centric, and it remains so even in the face of a growing flood of complex and unstructured enterprise-wide— that is, *inter*agency—challenges. Without a cadre of enterprise leaders, tackling the growing number of wicked government problems is likely to be hit or miss at best. This growing crisis in *enterprise* leadership and what to do about it is the focus of this book.

Just over a year ago, the Brookings Institution, through Brookings Executive Education and Olin Business School, and with the support of Booz Allen Hamilton, sponsored a symposium on the leadership challenges of wicked government problems. A small but eclectic group of leadership practitioners and scholars who had been thinking about that challenge came together in that symposium to examine the crisis. Their thoughts, now in the form of the chapters that follow, serve as a forum for how to address the current challenges of leading the federal enterprise. It is our hope, as well as the hope of the contributors to this book, that the forum stirs much discussion, debate, and, ultimately, progress.

In that regard, we would like to express our appreciation to our contributors, many of whom are "sitting" federal officials, for their compelling insights into the emerging theory and practice of enterprise leadership. We would also like to thank our respective employers—Olin Business School at Washington University in St. Louis for Dr. Nickerson and Booz Allen Hamilton for Dr. Sanders—for giving us the time and support to launch this discussion; without their generosity the book would not have been possible. It also would not have been possible without the tireless efforts of Dr. Rachel Mendelowitz, a Booz Allen Hamilton colleague, who along with Carolyn Mauriello, also of Booz Allen Hamilton, gave much of their own time to keep us all on track, in terms of both substance and process.

Tackling Wicked
Government
Problems

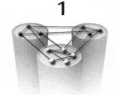

1

The Enterprise Leadership Challenge

JACKSON NICKERSON AND RONALD SANDERS

D o any of the following scenarios sound familiar?

—In the midst of a hurricane, communications and organizational breakdowns force a Coast Guard officer to step in and try to coordinate the disaster relief efforts of an alphabet soup of federal, state, and local agencies. The National Guard, a host of nongovernmental agencies like the Red Cross, and even citizen volunteers are all trying to do what is right but according to their own and often conflicting rules of engagement. And the only ones the officer actually commands are the relatively few uniformed "Coasties" who report directly to her.

—The Defense Department designates a senior federal executive as its official representative to an interagency task force charged with helping find work for thousands of veterans discharged at the end of more than a decade of war in Iraq and Afghanistan. He finds himself at the table with departments as diverse as Labor, Veterans Affairs, Education, and even the Small Business Administration, and he realizes that they do not even speak the same bureaucratic dialects, let alone see the challenge the same way.

—A CIA station chief somewhere in the Middle East looks at a critical piece of intelligence just handed to her by one of her case officers. It includes an obscure reference to an individual just returning from the United States on a tourist visa, and she needs to know exactly what he did (and whom he visited) while in Detroit. Distant in both geography and authority, she finds herself quickly needing to mobilize FBI agents in the Midwest to investigate.

—During a routine plant inspection, an Agriculture Department inspector finds a tainted piece of meat and evidence that it may be part of a larger shipment imported from the Far East several weeks ago. The rest of the shipment already is en route to processing plants and grocery stores all over the southeastern United States. Furthermore, indications suggest there is more meat from the supplier due to arrive in port in a few days. Investigating the current shipment requires a rapid response from not only several units within the Department of Agriculture but also from Customs and Border Protection agents at the port. His last experience with Customs and Border Protection was anything but rapid, requiring several hours on the phone.

These vignettes represent a growing reality in today's federal government. More and more of the challenges that government leaders face—from the drama of disaster to matters of meat inspection—extend beyond their narrowly authorized and specialized missions. In today's rapidly changing and chaotic world, the problems that government must address are increasingly complex, cross-jurisdictional, amorphous, and difficult to solve—what is commonly referred to as "wicked" problems.

We argue that wicked problems ultimately require enterprise solutions. "Enterprise" here refers to the resources and capabilities found in the constellation of public and private organizations that must act in concert if they are to successfully address cross-cutting national and international challenges. Such entities include federal, state, and local government agencies; tribal governments; private and not-for-profit organizations; and even international organizations like the United Nations, Interpol, and the International Monetary Fund.

Wicked challenges may be strategic and long-term, like global climate change, or they may be operational, like food safety and counterterrorism. In any case, while the contours and composition of the enterprise may vary depending on the situation, there is one common denominator: an enterprise consists of multiple organizations, each semiautonomous or independent, but with at least some overlapping common goal or interest in tackling a wicked problem.

The American public looks to the federal government to successfully respond to and resolve wicked problems, especially those that span the enterprise. Yet the current federal organizational structure is not well designed to provide such enterprise-wide responses; indeed, it may never be perfectly structured to deal with such problems if its operating environment continues to change rapidly and unpredictably. Given the size of the federal government and the substantial political and legal hurdles for redesigning and modifying structures and authorities, attempts to reconfigure the government, while needed, always will greatly lag behind these environmental changes. Organizational change may be a necessary response to environmental shifts, but with substantial inertia slowing such processes, structural responses always will be insufficient for providing enterprise-wide solutions to wicked problems.

If structural solutions are not sufficient, how then can the federal government respond to and resolve wicked problems? We argue that these challenges, both fleeting and enduring, require a new kind of leader and a new kind of leadership development approach. These challenges require a type of leader who understands that *tackling wicked government problems* requires building and drawing upon a network of critical organizational and individual actors, no matter where they may reside. They require a type of leader who can encourage and facilitate collaboration by leveraging shared values and interests to achieve a resolution that is greater than the sum of individual actions. We call individuals who are imbued with or have developed such abilities "enterprise leaders," and they are increasingly in demand.

Given the constraints of existing management authorities, governmental structures, and historical approaches to leadership development, many of today's government leaders simply are ill equipped to tackle wicked government problems. Put plainly, the government needs to substantially increase the number of enterprise leaders in its ranks, and to do so, it needs to change its paradigm for developing such leaders.

Recognizing that developing a new leadership paradigm is itself a wicked government problem, we reached out to a set of enterprise-wide actors—government executives, academics, think tanks, thought leaders, and consultants—to assemble a collaborative, interdisciplinary, and broadly experienced network of individuals with overlapping interests. Sponsored by Brookings Executive Education and Booz Allen Hamilton, we held a symposium at the Brookings Institution in March 2012 to discuss the issues of enterprise leadership and leading through collaborative networks. Participants were subsequently invited to write chapters to contribute to this edited volume.

The purpose of this book is to heighten recognition of the need for enterprise leadership, to explore alternative views of the capabilities needed to be an enterprise leader, and to highlight some early steps being taken by agencies to develop a new cadre of enterprise leaders.

The first part of book, "Contemporary Enterprise Leadership Challenges," focuses on the individuals who are charged (formally or otherwise) with tackling wicked problems. Our assumption is that, while these leaders are likely to be senior officials in one or more of the enterprise's constituent organizations, they will rarely have any sort of formal, chain of command authority over most of its constituent components, not to mention the enterprise as a whole. This is an all-too-common contradiction to the classic axiom that authority must match accountability. The second part, "What Makes for an Effective Enterprise Leader," offers several perspectives on various skills and capabilities required of successful enterprise leaders. The third part, "An Enterprise Approach to Leadership Development," describes several practical approaches implemented by federal agencies in their efforts to develop enterprise leaders.

We conclude the book by summarizing lessons learned from these contributors and laying out a bold alternative and practical guide for how to develop enterprise leaders. The following paragraphs provide an overview of the issues discussed in each of the three sections and briefly summarize the contribution of each chapter.

Part 1: Contemporary Enterprise Leadership Challenges

The definition of enterprise leadership is admittedly imprecise, in part because those of us who worry about the state of leadership in today's federal government are only now beginning to recognize the distinction and differences between leading an enterprise (as we have defined it) and leading an organization that by that definition is almost always going to be part of the larger whole. In so doing, we are also beginning to recognize the inadequacy of "traditional" leadership development strategies to prepare those who must lead that larger whole—sometimes by design but more often by default.

With some exceptions—most notably the U.S. military and, more recently, the U.S. intelligence community—the vast majority of leadership models and the development strategies that operationalize them implicitly assume that leaders function in an intraorganizational context, that is, they are embedded in a formal organizational structure with a defined mission, limits of authority, and accountability. While these formal structures are shaped by a culture as well as the informal organizational relationships that make leadership so interesting, even these intangibles are implicitly intraorganizational in nature. Actors (individual, organizational, and institutional) external to that formally and informally bounded structure are normally treated as part of the leader's external environment: important but implicitly extraorganizational, something to be aware of and to navigate through but largely outside the leader's sphere of influence.

To be sure, lots of boundaries exist internal to an organization—for example, between operating divisions and geographic units, line and staff functions like human resources and finance—and leaders are most certainly developed (in the classroom as well as on the job) to be aware of and operate across those internal boundaries. For the most part, however, these boundaries remain embedded in a larger formal structure (a company, an agency), and that larger structure is defined, in many cases legally and through authorities, by what is inside and outside the responsibility of the organization. Importantly, these organizations typically possess a clearly defined chain of command that stops with some official who is ultimately accountable for the performance of that organization and who serves as judge and jury for any internal, "cross-border" disputes between organizational units under their responsibility.

Such intraorganizational landscapes are important considerations for leaders in government today; after all, most of leadership's challenges originate in the immediate organizational environment. Leaders are developed in the classroom and on the job to effectively lead in their intraorganizational environment.

This approach is undoubtedly necessary, but it is no longer sufficient for those leaders who must confront wicked government problems that transcend organizational and institutional boundaries and span the greater enterprise. These wicked problems, which we believe are no longer exceptions, require a different kind of leader, one who can discern where their organization fits in the larger enterprise, is charged with comprehensively framing and formulating the wicked problem, and can bring together the networks of actors from across the enterprise who share an interest in resolving the wicked problem. To get a better grounding in the challenges of enterprise leadership, we turn to three enterprise leaders who share with us the wicked government problems they faced and how they responded to their enterprise challenges.

A former director of national intelligence, the Honorable J. Michael "Mike" McConnell, shares his story of how he was charged with unifying the intelligence community to work together as an enterprise (see chapter 2). In response to 9-11, his mission was to create a culture of "jointness" across various agencies responsible for our national security. McConnell, recognizing the importance of sharing information and leading thinking, had to counter the resistance of agencies to sharing information and did so by creating a "forcing function." He describes how he contributed to solving the wicked problem of sharing information and the lessons he learned throughout the process as he reshaped the institutional architecture of the intelligence community. McConnell reflects on how his enterprise leadership abilities were molded through networks, particularly informal networks, and how his connectedness to others across the government sector contributed to his success.

Pat Tamburrino (chapter 3) describes the impact enterprise leadership had as he served as the chief of staff to the under secretary of defense for personnel and readiness, when he partnered with the Department of Veterans Affairs (VA) and other agencies to maximize the career readiness of all servicemembers. The enterprise goal in his case was to reduce unemployment for veterans by giving them the support and resources they needed to enter the civilian workforce. With very different perspectives and missions, the Department of Defense, the VA, and the other agencies involved had to find common ground upon which to build and deliver a program to ease this transition. The chapter outlines four features of the delivery model and, more importantly, how agencies collaborated to accomplish their joint goal within a short period of time.

Finally, in chapter 4, Admiral Thad Allen, Leonard Marcus, and Barry Dorn discuss the concept of meta-leadership and its critical components and their impacts in the aftermath of Hurricane Katrina and the Deepwater Horizon oil spill. Dorn and Marcus, both affiliated with the Harvard School of Public Health, have conducted research and developed the concepts and practices associated with meta-leadership, which offers a mindset for managing a complex catastrophic disaster well. This approach contributes to enterprise leadership by describing how a leader faced with such a challenge can unify and leverage the agencies, organizations, and people that are involved. The chapter goes on to describe five essential dimensions of meta-leadership practice: the leader, the situation, leading down, leading up, and leading across.

Part 2: What Makes for an Effective Enterprise Leader?

The first part of the book offers examples of the challenges that face enterprise leaders and hints at some of the qualities and competencies necessary for success. The second part of this book asks, "What makes for an effective enterprise leader?" To start, the enterprise leader needs to identify and understand the missions, structures, budgets, and bureaucratic processes of all relevant enterprise actors. But this knowledge is only the beginning; enterprise leaders must also understand and appreciate their histories, cultures, traditions, stories, "heroes," and lore—in other words, their DNA—in order to empathetically see the enterprise's shared challenge through the "eyes" of each actor.

Second, understanding the depth and breadth of information, knowledge, and motivation of the enterprise actors, the enterprise leader needs to engage the relevant network of actors so that they comprehensively and collectively see and understand the wicked problem. Framing and formulating the wicked challenge often depends on the dynamic social system, with complex formal and informal interrelationships and interdependencies, positive and negative feedback loops, and so on that exist between and among the directly relevant actors, organizations, and institutions. This understanding needs to extend to how the relevant enterprise actors interact with the broader institutional environment.

Third, the enterprise leader needs to engage the relevant network of enterprise actors in developing and implementing a comprehensive and feasible solution without formal authority and well beyond his or her chain of command. The use of commitment instead of command is a quality that helps to distinguish the enterprise leader from more traditionally trained and more internally focused leaders, for while they too must be able to exercise influence over peers and colleagues of equal stature and rank, they typically do so in the context of a shared chain of command that ultimately leads to the head of the agency or department—where the buck stops. In most cases, the enterprise leader enjoys no such luxury.

With few exceptions, today's federal departments and agencies operate as semiautonomous stovepipes (or as one official described them, "cylinders of excellence"), with separate missions, budgets, and congressional oversight. And, while constitutionally all government leaders and their organizations report to the president, there is no such practical reality. Add state and local governments, international organizations, nongovernmental organizations, and the private sector into the mix, and there is no way to "delegate leadership upward."

Without effective enterprise leadership, interagency impasses often fester, or worse, become muddled and mired in the search for a lowest-common-denominator consensus among actors who will not budge. Experienced enterprise leaders have (sometimes painfully) learned to focus on building upon shared interests and a sense of common mission, or the bond of shared values and experiences. They have learned to leverage those commitments through networks of trusted extraorganizational relationships or a personal reservoir of social capital built and employed to achieve the ends of the enterprise.

This ability to build and leverage boundary-spanning networks is a common theme in the case studies of enterprise leadership, which suggests that much can be learned from the science of organizational network analysis. To explore what makes for an effective enterprise leader, we turn to four researchers to understand how they think about this still-emerging notion of enterprise leadership.

In chapter 5, Jackson Nickerson, a chaired professor at Olin Business School and director of Brookings' Executive Education program, discusses strategies for enterprise leadership through network governance. He explains how Rick Thomas, of the Department of Defense's Test Resource Management Center, improved the management of U.S. missile ranges by coordinating and collaborating across a network of thirty-three different agencies that lacked a central authority. Nickerson highlights four practical components of network governance through which enterprise leaders tackle wicked government problems: establishing language and communication channels, building and maintaining trust and reputation among collaborating actors and entities, balancing dependence so that one organization is not at significantly more at risk than the other, and determining mutual incentives or common goals that encourage collaborative action.

Rob Cross, an associate professor at the University of Virginia's McIntire School of Commerce, and his coauthors, Andrew Hargadon, professor of technology management at the University of California, Davis, and Salvatore Parise, associate professor at Babson College in the Technology, Operations, and Information Management Division, introduce in chapter 6 the idea that innovation is not always the result of an individual effort but instead often arises from a collaborative effort that organizations can foster by focusing on using expertise at the critical points of need. The integration of multiple great ideas and technologies can be achieved through informal networks that allow for innovation. Cross, Hargadon, and Parise discuss the three main challenges to innovation: fragmentation, domination, and insularity. They then propose five practices for using networks to drive innovation and recommend they be applied in a holistic way. Governments face many challenges in innovation, but it is critical that they adapt to their environment. By learning to collaborate, agencies can overcome barriers to innovation and survive in today's complex environment.

Thomas Valente, an associate professor at the University of Southern California Department of Preventive Medicine, discusses in chapter 7 the detrimental effects of organizational silos and the benefits of a network-oriented perspective. He demonstrates the difference between formal and informal networks and relationships and the far-reaching effects that informal relationships can have on an organization. Using computer simulations, Valente shows the impact of networked leaders, who use a relational approach instead of one based on more formal authority. His results illustrate how silos slow the spread of information, and how by using opinion leaders and meaningful ways of creating networks, enterprise leaders can be much more effective.

In chapter 8, Donna Chrobot-Mason, associate professor at the University of Cincinnati, and her colleagues Kristin Cullen and David Altman, from the Center for Creative Leadership, offer a boundary spanning leadership model as a guide for addressing problems that require intergroup collaboration. While their approach seems counterintuitive, Chrobot-Mason and her colleagues have found that boundaries must first be managed before they are spanned. Leaders first must encourage groups to define their own strengths, values, and responsibilities so that when they collaborate with others, they can do so in a constructive way that maintains group identity. Once groups find common ground, leaders can help them work together more effectively by establishing a shared mission and encouraging connections at the individual level. Finally, Chrobot-Mason, Cullen, and Altman describe how leaders can guide their groups into new frontiers by integrating differences to achieve a common mission or transform the groups by identifying a new direction and collective joint values and beliefs.

Part 3: An Enterprise Approach to Leadership Development

The qualities of enterprise leadership rarely are included in formal agency leadership development programs, which are implicitly inwardly biased. Far more often than not, enterprise leadership qualities, to the extent that they exist, evolve incidentally and most often are learned on the job through a series of trials and errors involving the proverbial school of hard knocks. The costs of developing enterprise leaders in such a way is immense because using trial and error to solve wicked problems not only makes success unlikely but also increases solution fatigue, cynicism, and mistrust with each unsuccessful trial. What is needed is a more disciplined and deliberate way to develop enterprise leaders.

The third part of the book calls upon government leadership development experts to describe some of the approaches they have advocated, or in some cases taken, to develop enterprise leaders. Some of these strategies are already in practice; thus, while they may be nascent in many respects, they do offer some initial steps forward.

In chapter 9, Jim Trinka, former chief learning officer at the FBI, shares the lessons he learned in the Department of Veterans Affairs as executive director for Leading EDGE (Executives Driving Government Excellence), a program that facilitates cross-agency collaboration and, implicitly, the development of enterprise leaders. Trinka identifies systemic barriers that make enterprise leadership difficult to develop and execute: a culture that views collaboration as a short-lived event rather than a lasting relationship, departments competing for limited resources and talent, the prevalence of short-term appointees with limited time and relationships to leverage for interagency efforts, and a lack of training to develop executives' enterprise leadership competencies, skills, and attitudes. The VA has invested in one such leadership development program with Leading EDGE and has reaped tangible benefits as a result.

Chapter 10, by Ron Sanders, vice president and fellow at Booz Allen Hamilton and former associate director of national intelligence, discusses the impetus for developing an enterprise-focused approach to leader development in the intelligence community following the intelligence failure of 9-11. Sanders provides an overview of the challenges overcome by the Office of the Director of National Intelligence (ODNI) as it spearheaded the intelligence community's civilian joint duty program in an effort to develop enterprise leaders. Overcoming substantial bureaucratic resistance to the program, the ODNI and leaders of other intelligence agencies collaboratively determined what would qualify as joint duty, how employees would be selected and evaluated, and how to handle other operational concerns. Sanders provides lessons learned from the multiyear effort, including the importance of establishing clear administrative and operational guidelines, providing proper incentives, and strongly engaging senior leadership.

In chapter 11, Laura Miller Craig and Jessica Nierenberg of the Government Accountability Office draw conclusions from government surveys and research reports that indicate interagency job rotation has proven successful in developing enterprise leaders. In one survey, 86 percent of participants in rotation programs found their experience to be "very effective" in helping them develop skills necessary for leading in an interagency environment. Designing and managing interagency programs is not without its challenges; however, Miller Craig and Nierenberg offer strategies for successfully implementing rotation programs. Among other things, they argue that agency and individual goals should be aligned, and incentives must be implemented to encourage participation. The U.S. Army Command and General Staff College Interagency Fellowship Program illustrates how these strategies can be used to establish a successful program and develop enterprise leaders.

Finally, in chapter 12, Stephen T. Shih, deputy associate director of the Senior Executive Service (SES) and performance management at the U.S. Office of Personnel Management, discusses strategies for developing an executive corps of enterprise leaders at the seniormost levels of the federal government. Since its inception in 1978, the SES has become increasingly agency specific, with a focus on technical, rather than leadership capabilities. However, Shih argues that to solve today's wicked problems, the SES must return to developing a cadre of enterprise leaders, able to provide government-wide vision and produce results through interagency collaboration. Whether through a centralized, top-down, management system or a decentralized management structure in which individuals coordinate enterprise collaboration, the government's senior executives must be recruited, selected, developed, and managed to emphasize enterprise leadership capabilities.

Conclusion: The Key to Developing Enterprise Leaders

To conclude this book, we reflect on the contributions of the various authors and offer our assessment of what we think are the key and pragmatic insights on how to develop enterprise leaders on a large scale. We note that there is no single "silver bullet" strategy that guarantees the development of enterprise leaders; rather, we believe a variety of approaches and methods are available, some easy and relatively low cost to implement while others require breaking existing paradigms of leadership development. Whatever the approach, we believe that there are several key ingredients that are critical to success, which we enumerate in the concluding chapter. All of the success factors we identify will require considerable enterprise-wide focus, commitment, and effort to change. However, we believe that these changes are feasible and necessary to develop the enterprise leadership the nation needs to tackle wicked government problems.

PART **I**
*Contemporary Enterprise
Leadership Challenges*

2

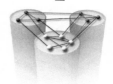

Leading the National Security Enterprise: Some Personal Observations

J. MICHAEL MCCONNELL

The need for leaders who can reach across organizational boundaries, unify the efforts of multiple agencies, and drive them to achieve results—in other words, what this book defines as enterprise leaders—has never been more apparent. I saw this firsthand as our country's second director of national intelligence (DNI), where I was charged by Congress and the commander in chief to make the U.S. Intelligence Community (IC) actually act like one. In the aftermath of 9-11, this was not just an academic exercise—it was a national security imperative.

A History Lesson

However, this was not the first time the nation needed the kind of leaders who could break down and break out of their organizational stovepipes, who could subsume their parochial interests to the greater good, and who, in so doing, could get big things done—in other words: enterprise leaders. Nor was this the first time that U.S. national security depended on such leadership.

One of the times the United States realized that it needed enterprise leaders was back in the early 1980s. For years Barry Goldwater, the five-term U.S. senator from Arizona, had been convinced that the United States would be more effective against its enemies if the Department of Defense were empowered to force its four military branches to act in a more integrated, seamless way, that is, jointly. He and his like-minded "revolutionaries" worked to pass legislation codifying something called joint duty for the U.S. military, but they faced fierce opposition from the services, and by 1983 they still had nothing to show for it.

Then there was that little dustup in a place called Grenada, where the Cubans were trying to expand their presence. When the United States took exception to that, the Cubans seized some hostages (including some Americans), and the U.S. government decided to send to troops to rescue them. This is precisely what the U.S. military was supposed to be able to do: be ready to go anytime, anywhere, for a show of force or to conduct successful military operations. And that's exactly what the armed forces did, deploying about 7,600 troops to Grenada, including the U.S. Army's Rapid Deployment Force, the Marines, Army Delta Force, and Navy SEALs.

But there was a little problem: the Cubans were holding out, and the U.S. troops on the ground had no way to talk to each other. The army took one side of the island and the marines took the other. At the time, a marine radio could not be used to communicate with an army radio. Lieutenants from each side had to hike out to find the nearest pay phone, so that a marine lieutenant could call Camp Lejeune and an army officer could call Fort Bragg, and they could be patched together over commercial telephone lines so they could discuss what was supposed to be a "joint" operation.

As the story is told, when this information got back to Goldwater, he was furious and determined more than ever to pass a bill that forced the services to become joint. Every service chief and every service secretary told him that if he passed such a bill, it would cause great harm to the U.S. military. But with Grenada fresh on his mind, he pushed the bill through anyway. The Goldwater-Nichols Act passed the Senate and the House, and over the unanimous objections of the services, President Ronald Reagan signed it into law on October 1, 1986.

The Goldwater-Nichols Act changed the structure and culture of the Defense Department overnight. The structural changes got all the headlines. It streamlined the chain of command by cutting out all of the service secretaries and service chiefs so that the president and the secretary of defense could reach directly to the regionally organized combatant commands responsible for "jointly" deploying air, land, and sea forces.

However, in my opinion, the act's impact on the culture of the U.S. military was far more important. Its goal was to create a culture of jointness, and its lever to achieve that goal was the ultimate incentive: promotion to general officer. The act required all lieutenants, lieutenant commanders and lieutenant colonels, and colonels who aspired to be a general or an admiral (including me) to become "joint certified" by completing a joint duty assignment in one of those regional combatant commands or something similar. Once the bill passed, the services realized that if they were going to go to war, it was going to be jointly and not as individual services, and individual members realized that the only path to becoming a general officer was through joint certification.

I will always remember going to Capitol Hill with then chairman of the joint chiefs General Colin Powell as his J-2 (the joint staff's chief intelligence officer) after Desert Shield–Desert Storm and seeing every service chief under oath testifying that Goldwater-Nichols and jointness were the best thing to ever happen to the U.S. military.

The Importance of a Forcing Function

What was true of the armed services then is the reality today across many public and private sector organizations: there is a fundamental need for leaders who can think beyond their immediate organization and act jointly on behalf of the larger enterprise. Another reality is the inevitable bureaucratic resistance to that mindset, especially when it comes to sharing information and collaborating across organizational boundaries. It is not that groups are not interested in getting information from others; they just are reluctant to share their own. According to the old adage, information is power: if you have it, you have a position of power; if you give it away, there is a perceived loss of power.

If we want enterprise-focused leaders to be collaborative, we cannot just tell them to start acting that way. There has to be a forcing function. For instance, when I left the National Security Agency in 1996 and joined a management and technology consulting firm, I found an organization whose leaders did not think and act like an enterprise; instead, the firm was beset by destructive internal competition, and the firm's leadership deliberately set out to change that.

One of the forcing functions used was the 360-degree performance review. This entails 360-degree feedback gathered from one's boss, subordinates, colleagues, and clients, and it is traditionally used only for developmental purposes. However, at my firm, those reviews were given real "teeth" by making them part of a leader's annual performance evaluation.

As this practice was instituted across the firm, it became apparent that the approach was driving the firm's collaborative culture. If an individual was not collaborative, it would come out during the annual performance review, and the individual was expected to change his or her behavior by the time of the next annual appraisal.

That is why, to this day, my firm fosters a culture where leaders encourage, model, and reward collaboration and information-sharing across all of the firm's business units, and the insights that come from that collaboration have been invaluable to the firm's clients.

I took that experience with me when I returned to government as DNI in 2007, and I immediately set out to instill that same "culture of collaboration" into the IC. Among other things, my office implemented a civilian version of military joint duty that was designed to develop and deploy enterprise leaders throughout the intelligence community.

That turned out to be a two-year bureaucratic battle, but after it was implemented, I assumed that the IC would embrace complementary ideas like 360-degree performance reviews that rewarded collaborative, enterprise leadership. I was wrong; many of the IC's senior leadership roundly rejected the idea of 360-degree reviews other than for developmental purposes.

I was surprised at the pushback, but it helped me realize that if I wanted to reshape the way intelligence-gathering agencies shared information and collaborated, I was going to have to leverage all of the networks of trusted relationships I had built over my years of government service to persuade those agencies to think and act like an intelligence enterprise.

The Fight over Executive Order 12333

One of the vehicles I tried to use in that regard was Executive Order (EO) 12333, which President Reagan signed in 1981. That document is considered the Bible for running the U.S. intelligence community—in fact, it actually defines that community and establishes the institutional relationships between its member agencies. However, it was conceived during the cold war, and the world had changed dramatically since its original issuance. This was particularly the case with respect to threats to our national security and the corresponding missions of the IC.

The Intelligence Reform and Terrorism Prevention Act (IRTPA) of 2004 was an attempt to respond to those changes, but it also added another layer of complexity. Among other things, it established the Office of the Director of National Intelligence (ODNI) to oversee the IC, which brought to seventeen the total number of agencies, groups, and organizations conducting the nation's intelligence work.

However, in bringing together those seventeen agencies and organizations, IRTPA did not go far enough. Fifteen of those entities (the two exceptions were the ODNI and the Central Intelligence Agency) reported to six different cabinet officers and therefore had their own internal reporting relationships. They also were subject to separate congressional oversight and authorization processes. As a result, their relationship to the ODNI was unclear.

There are three words in government that determine the nature of those interagency relationships: direction, control, and authority. When one agency or agency official has direction, control, and authority over another, it assumes a superior-subordinate relationship with that other organization or official. In other words, one can command the other to do its bidding.

Yet, when Congress drafted and passed the IRTPA, it neglected to use those words when describing the relationship between the ODNI and the other intelligence agencies that constituted the IC. Because of those missing words, the act set up an inherent tension between the ODNI and the sixteen "subordinate" agencies it was tasked with overseeing.

When I entered the picture as the DNI in 2007, I was immediately seen as an interloper (this despite my career as an intelligence officer), upsetting the balance of power in a process that had been in equilibrium for years. The IC agencies knew who they reported to, and now suddenly they were no longer sure. I did not share their uncertainty. The whole reason the ODNI was created was because of the intelligence failings leading up to 9-11.

The purpose of the IC is to identify threats and take action to prevent tragedies like that from occurring. So when 9-11 happened, by definition the IC failed. One of the stress points of that failure was the stovepiped organizational structure and insular relationships that had characterized the IC for so long. The IRTPA was intended to fix that, but because of the vagaries of the legislative process, it fell short, and the ODNI was left in bureaucratic limbo as a result. It became clear to me that to escape that limbo, EO 12333 needed to be redone, and with it, the IC's institutional architecture.

I made the case for changing EO 12333, and everyone agreed; there was no question that it was outdated and needed to be modernized to reflect the IC's new reality. However, there was little agreement, especially at the outset, about what those changes should look like—especially regarding any changes that infringed on the "direction, control, and authority" of the IC's many agencies. As one would expect, as soon as we started down that path, the lawyers came out of the woodwork to "protect the prerogatives" of their respective secretaries, and the resistance was overwhelming.

That resistance centered on the sharing of information and intelligence. Arguably, the failure of the IC's agencies to do so led to 9-11, but those agencies argued just as vehemently that sharing information could also put lives at risk by compromising their sources and thus their ability to obtain secret intelligence in the future. But the real underlying rationale for their resistance was, "We may lose something. We may lose some of our 'authority' over who controls those secrets, and who can direct their dissemination." This was a real dilemma: if there was too little information sharing, the enterprise's agencies could not connect the dots and act as one to confront a threat; but too much sharing could lead to the disclosure of secrets, with consequences just as tragic.

The Power of Trust

Having been an intelligence officer for almost my entire professional life, I saw this as a false dichotomy, one that was at odds with my mission as DNI. If the IC were to act as an enterprise, its members needed to share information and intelligence as one team with one fight. I knew that one of the ways to accomplish that mission would be to rework EO 12333. However, given the resistance to that effort, I concluded that my only chance for success was to work outside the bureaucracy and enlist the capabilities of my own network of trusted relationships, some from years past, others more recently established.

So the institutional battle was joined: the DNI versus the rest of the IC and their parent cabinet departments. I was clearly outnumbered, but fortunately, this was not going to be settled by a vote. The final decisionmaker in all of this would be the president of the United States. After all, he would ultimately sign a revised executive order, so I knew that if I could win him over, I had a chance. I did not have the kind of personal relationship with President George W. Bush that I had with his National Security Advisor Stephen Hadley or White House Chief of Staff Joshua Bolten, and since there was no time to build one, I looked for people that the president already knew and trusted. I reasoned that if I could find and win them over, there would be a much better chance of success.

I found them on the President's Intelligence Advisory Board. In the run-up to my nomination and confirmation as DNI, I had come to know this group, which serves as an independent source of advice and counsel to the president on intelligence matters. During that process, it became clear to me that they shared my commitment to making the IC into a true enterprise, and just as important, there were members on the board who were very close to the president—they had grown up with him, gone to college with him—and he trusted them to give him unvarnished recommendations.

At my urging, they had a private session with the president in which they told him of my cause and the bureaucratic obstacles that were standing in the way. As soon as his close contacts made the case, the president said, "Let's do it. Call a cabinet meeting and I'll tell the department heads I want this done." In July 2008, President Bush issued Executive Order 13470, which revised EO 12333 and gave the DNI greater *administrative* control over the intelligence community. It could not (and did not) go as far as the IRTPA could have; that would have required another act of Congress, and no one was confident that Congress would agree. However, it went far enough to serve as the foundation for a true intelligence enterprise.

Most important, it shifted the "burden of (bureaucratic) proof" in disagreements regarding the reach of DNI authority over the IC's agencies. Before the new executive order, it was assumed that the cabinet departments inherently had that authority, and the DNI had to prove otherwise to them to act. With EO 13470, the president gave the DNI the authority to act *unless* a department could prove that the action would infringe on its prerogatives. Given that the president was the final arbiter in those disagreements, the odds were in the DNI's favor.

Ultimately, that network of trusted associates was able to achieve what I did not have the legal or political capacity to do on my own: transcend bureaucratic barriers and make the case for change directly to the president. And with the issuance of EO 13470, the ODNI was finally able to get the agencies to collaborate on an operational level and begin acting like an enterprise, without changing any existing legal authorities.

This experience provides a critical lesson for any government manager who is charged with leading an interagency effort: when organizational stovepipes get in your way, you must be able to build and leverage networks of trusted relationships that can bridge or break down those boundaries to enable action at an enterprise level.

There are a host of other qualities that I think distinguish great leaders from merely capable ones. But in today's operating environment, where almost everything has an "inter" (interagency, intergovernmental, international) element to it, I strongly believe it is the ability of leaders to work across organizational boundaries that sets them apart. Successful enterprise leaders are those who can overcome bureaucratic barriers to get meaningful interagency work done—and they do so by being connected. They build and then tap their network of trusted interorganizational relationships to win support for their objectives. And when those networks do not provide access to those with influence, enterprise leaders work to build new ones that do and then connect through them.

I agree wholeheartedly with the premise of this book that the most significant challenges government faces today will not be solved by individual agencies but by interagency cooperation across and outside of the bureaucratic chain of formal command. My whole career has been shaped by informal networks, and much of my success has been because of them. I am encouraged that the next generation of leaders has begun to recognize how important connectedness will be, not just to their own careers but to our nation's future.

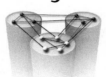

3

Collaborating to Honor Our Veterans

PASQUALE (PAT) M. TAMBURRINO JR.

In August 2011, President Barack Obama called on the Departments of Defense (DOD) and Veterans Affairs (VA) to lead an interagency task force in close consultation with White House policy councils and other federal agencies, including the Department of Labor (DOL), the Department of Education, and the Office of Personnel Management, to develop proposals to maximize the career readiness of all servicemembers. This DOD-VA Veterans Employment Initiative Task Force is one element of the president's comprehensive plan to support our nation's veterans and provide the assistance they need to transition from military to civilian life while at the same time reducing the veteran unemployment rate.

In today's rapidly changing job market, with companies operating under fiscal constraints and increased competition for high-quality jobs, it is more important than ever to prepare our separating servicemembers for the transition to civilian life. Nearly 90 percent of the individuals who left the services in 2012 were under the age of thirty-five. All of them will need to decide what their second career will be, and as veterans, they may face unique challenges in making this transition. However, a significant investment has been put into each and every departing service-member, and as a result exiting veterans have top-notch training, education, and experience. The president recognizes not only our commitment as a nation to support their sacrifice but also our need to derive a return on our investment by getting these veterans back into the workforce. The veteran unemployment rate has been on the decrease; the 2012 annual rate of 7.6 percent was below the national unemployment rate of 7.9 percent. However, the unemployment rate for younger veterans at the end of 2012 was nearly triple that, at 20.4 percent. On average, 300,000 veterans separate from the services each year; this does not include the troops expected to separate following the drawdown from Afghanistan. It is imperative the DOD, VA, and all partner agencies work together to better prepare these skilled workers for the transition into the second phase of their lives, an undertaking that will also strengthen our nation's workforce.

To meet the president's call for a "career-ready military," the DOD-VA Veterans Employment Initiative Task Force proposed a new transition assistance program to better facilitate the service-member's transition from military to civilian life. This transition model has four key features.

The first feature is designed to establish career readiness standards for all servicemembers (of both active and reserve components). These career readiness standards are part of the Individual Transition Plan that will ensure the individual meets all the requirements needed for job applications, training program acceptance, and the like. The standards are currently under review but will be common across military departments and all transition programs.

The second feature provides servicemembers with a set of value-added, individually tailored training programs and services to give them the set of tools they need to successfully transition. In the near term, it will institute a modular, outcome-based training curriculum, called Transition GPS (Goals, Planning, and Success), that will be implemented by all the military services, with support from the VA and DOL and tailored to the individual servicemembers' needs. This curriculum, which would build on the existing Transition Assistance Program (TAP), will be managed by the individual services and executed with VA and DOL participation. In recognition of the increased numbers of service members that will be departing the military in the coming years, implementing this revised program quickly is the top priority.

The third feature will be added in future implementation of the program. Career readiness will become a part of the servicemember's entire military career. A military life cycle transition model will incorporate career readiness and transition preparation into the entire span of a servicemember's career, from accession to postmilitary civilian life. Thus, the transition program will no longer be designed solely for the end-of-career phase.

The last feature is the standardized end-of-military career "capstone" event, which verifies that the transitioning servicemember meets the established career readiness standards and is indeed "career ready." The capstone event primarily complements the training that the servicemember has received by providing any additional instruction or assistance needed.

The Challenge

On November 21, 2012, the revised TAP program was fully implemented throughout the Department of Defense. TAP is expected to reach approximately 250,000 transitioning members at 206 military installations each year for the foreseeable future. This integrated effort was conceived, designed, tested, and deployed within just fifteen months of the president's August 2011 call for action. The effort involved four cabinet-level agencies—the Departments of Defense, Veterans Affairs, Labor, and Education—plus the support of the Office of Personnel Management and the Small Business Administration. Because of the diverse agency interaction and the desire to take action quickly, several key issues had to be addressed: recognition of each agency's assigned mission, agreement on common language, and commitment to a common end state and an active governance structure. Each of these challenges was addressed in a proactive manner to deliver a revised program in support of our nation's servicemembers.

Understanding the Mission

Each of the involved agencies has a distinct mission, but that does not preclude common interests. For example, DOD's mission is "to provide military forces needed to deter war and to protect the security of our country."[1] The VA's mission focuses on President Lincoln's promise "'to care for him who shall have borne the battle, and for his widow, and his orphan' by serving and honoring the men and women who are America's veterans."[2] The connection between the military forces needed to protect national security and the welfare of those forces is self-evident. The mission of the DOL is to "to foster, promote, and develop the welfare of the wage earners, job seekers, and retirees of the United States; improve working conditions; advance opportunities for profitable employment; and assure work-related benefits and rights."[3] The VA and DOL missions overlap since both are involved with the support and well-being of current and former servicemembers. The mission of the Department of Education relates to all the above missions by aiming "to promote student achievement and preparation for global competitiveness by fostering educational excellence and ensuring equal access."[4]

Thus, despite their distinct missions, the agencies' common goal is to provide the means and resources needed for American men and women to contribute to the nation's global competitiveness, whether militarily, educationally, or economically. Each agency works to assist people in their desired endeavors. Servicemembers leaving the military, whether they exit after their first term of enlistment or after a career of twenty-plus years, have decisions to make. The most basic decision is what do they do next? This is the place where all agency missions align, in supporting this decision.

In the revised Transition Assistance Program, each agency collaborates in a unique way to address the many choices a separating servicemember faces, from caring for family to pursuing education to finding employment. To meet these needs, the agencies coordinated a modular training curriculum, based on standard outcomes and learning objectives, that is matched to the individual needs of servicemembers. This curriculum is referred to as Transition GPS (Goals, Planning, and Success). Requiring approximately one week to deliver the core materials, Transition GPS provides a coherent set of mandatory preseparation activities that includes DOD-administered preseparation counseling, VA benefits counseling and registration, and a DOL employment workshop. There are also three optional tracks that provide tailored skills building for each servicemember depending on the individual's desire to seek employment, pursue formal education, acquire technical training, or embark on an entrepreneurial career after separation.

During the mandatory preseparation counseling, servicemembers are briefed on VA benefits, including enrollment in eBenefits and MyHealtheVet.[5] In the optional tracks, DOL provides a comprehensive workshop to equip those who intend to transition directly into the labor market with all the tools they need to conduct a successful job search. The Department of Education also participates in the optional tracks by implementing a curriculum directed at those who intend to pursue college education. This curriculum features two days of counseling and preparation for the college application process.

The Task Force recognizes the critical importance of maintaining and enhancing linkages between the services and the tools provided by the various departments and agencies involved. For example, the Veterans Job Bank, hosted on the joint DOD-VA National Resource Directory, and the VA for Vets Career Center allow servicemembers and veterans to connect with thousands of "veteran-friendly" positions that are currently available from private sector employers and corporations as well as from the federal government.[6] DOL's "My Next Move for Veterans" is an interactive tool that helps veterans learn about their career options.[7]

To maximize its engagement, each agency had to fulfill its usual tasks in nontraditional ways. For example, the Department of Education traditionally focuses its attention on students in the K-12 range; however, recognizing its stake in the veteran transition process, the department shifted its efforts toward helping adult learners and accommodating their educational needs. The VA departed from its paradigm of assisting only post-service veterans by allowing current servicemembers access to VA systems prior to their discharge date. Early contact and familiarization with the VA ensures a smoother handoff of the member from active duty systems to systems focused on the veteran. Finally, DOL undertook a tremendous effort to reach into the services and help veterans clearly understand the value of their military skills in the civilian marketplace, vastly improving their employment opportunities.

The Need for a Common Language

Individuals with a wide range of experiences and professions, such as health care experts, financial planners, social workers, learning specialists, and information technology planners and designers, made up the Task Force and various teams. Although everyone was working toward the common goal of developing a new Transition Assistance Program, each of the agencies involved had a culture that had its own language, with all of its associated subtleties. In order to effectively communicate each team's intentions, a terms of reference document was created to establish the overall mission and desired outcomes. Specifically, this document put all desired outcomes in common terms that transcend unique functional areas and enable essential common understanding. This document not only helped to ensure that each team was operating with common terms, but ultimately it set an agreed upon end state that everyone was working toward.

Governance

The Task Force was guided by an exceptional senior executive–general officer–flag officer steering group that met weekly for well over a year. These senior leaders demonstrated a vested interest in the outcome of the Task Force by remaining engaged and active. The Task Force Executive Steering Group provided two key functions. First, it allowed cross-agency communications to flow in a timely fashion, up to and including the secretary of each department. This approach ensures that issues are addressed at the right level in a timely manner. Second, a forum of this type establishes clear intent, direction, and access, which facilitates execution by all other participants.

Conclusions

The DOD-VA Veterans Employment Initiative Task Force offers an example of successful interagency collaboration. Members of the Task Force from DOD, VA, DOL, and Department of Education broke through common barriers to interagency collaboration to develop an integrated framework for veteran transition to the civilian workforce.

This was achieved by each agency using its existing strengths and resources nontraditionally. The Task Force established a common language that allowed each agency to translate its terminology and acronyms into terms that the entire group could understand. The agencies agreed to collaborate around one clearly stated goal that encompassed the subgoals of each agency. Finally, agencies developed an effective governance structure led by an executive steering group that remained engaged and disseminated information quickly.

The government's largest, most complex problems often require crosscutting solutions that draw on the input and strengths of multiple agencies. With limited time and resources, enterprise leaders must collaborate across agency lines in pursuit of a common goal. While interagency issues may differ in complexity and scope, enterprise leaders can replicate the success of the DOD-VA Veterans Employment Initiative Task Force to solve problems better, faster, and with less operational cost.

Notes

1. Department of Defense, "About the Department of Defense (DOD)" (www.defense.gov/about/#mission).

2. Department of Veterans Affairs, "Mission, Vision, Core Values and Goals" (www.va.gov/about_va/mission.asp).

3. Department of Labor, "Our Mission" (www.dol.gov/opa/aboutdol/mission.htm).

4. Department of Education, "About ED: Overview and Mission Statement" (www2.ed.gov/about/landing.jhtml).

5. My HealtheVet is the VA online health website and portal, which offers veterans, active duty servicemembers, and their dependents and caregivers Internet access to VA health care information and services, including enrollment when eligible. My HealtheVet offers a free, online personal health record that empowers veterans to become informed partners in their health care. Servicemembers and veterans can access secure and current health and benefits information as well as record and store important health and military service information. Details on how this will be enabled will be provided in the implementation plan. See www.myhealth.va.gov/ index.html.

6. See, respectively, www.nrd.gov/home/veterans_job_bank, and http://vaforvets.va.gov/careercenter/pages/default.aspx.

7. The My Next Move website (www.mynextmove.org/vets/) has tasks, skills, salary information, job listings, and more for over 900 different careers.

4

Meta-Leadership in Concept and in Practice: The 2010 Gulf Oil Spill and 2005 Hurricane Katrina Response

LEONARD MARCUS, THAD ALLEN,
AND BARRY DORN

In times of crisis, there are leaders whose scope of thinking, capacity for unifying influence, and quality of timely performance extend far beyond their formal or expected bounds of authority. We call such people *meta-leaders,* and their characteristics and competencies can teach us much about how enterprise leaders can tackle "wicked problems" that are more enduring and persistent.

During a complex catastrophic disaster, these meta-leaders are able to marshal resources and direct action that is both comprehensive and cohesive. They integrate and thereby leverage an extensive range of agencies, organizations, and people—in other words, the many elements of the extended federal enterprise that are part of a disaster response—into informally coordinated but deliberate and decisive activity. This unity of effort is not limited to designated government agencies within the official chain of command. It also encompasses political leaders at all levels of government, large corporate as well as small businesses, community agencies, and members of the public that are mobilized into purposeful action.

This chapter is based on a March 7, 2012, presentation by the three coauthors at the Brookings Institution symposium entitled "The Power of Connectedness."

During a major disaster—such as the 2010 Deepwater Horizon Gulf oil spill or the aftereffects of the 2005 Hurricane Katrina response—a significant breadth of carefully coordinated enterprise-wide activity is necessary to mitigate the environmental and population impacts.

Meta-leaders rally people not merely because they have formal authority and sanctioned command powers. Above and beyond their core leadership attributes and technical capabilities, they convey respected proficiency, confidence in the face of crisis, emotional intelligence, and compassionate risk communication. They chart a meaningful direction and inspire, motivate, and direct others. In sum, they have influence in addition to and often well beyond their formal authority.

There are five dimensions of meta-leadership strategy and practice—derived through field observation and analysis of leaders in high-stakes, high-pressure crisis situations—that describe and guide these people and serve as an organizing framework for understanding the performance necessary to effectively lead the extended federal enterprise through complex disaster responses. This chapter provides an overview and description of the concepts and methods of meta-leadership and a narrative of how they applied to Admiral Thad Allen's leadership experience during the 2010 Deepwater Horizon oil spill and 2005 Hurricane Katrina responses. During both those responses, Admiral Allen met with and was interviewed in the field by Leonard Marcus and Barry Dorn. Given its short length, this chapter intends to provide a description, though not instruction, about meta-leadership.

Dimensions and Mindset of Meta-Leadership Practice

The five dimensions of meta-leadership practice comprise the *person of the leader* and his or her character, self-awareness, self-discipline, and effective role modeling for others; *the situation*—the problem, change, or crisis that compels immediate action or response, or the hazard that demands effective preparedness; *leading down* to one's organizational base and operating effectively in one's designated purview of authority; *leading up* to bosses or those to whom one is accountable, including elected and politically appointed officials; and *leading across* to other entities and organizations beyond one's immediate scope of authority to build system connectivity. That fifth dimension is most closely associated with this book's definition of enterprise, and as a consequence, we concentrate on that aspect of our model. In that regard, meta-leadership is particularly valuable when addressing major crises that demand that different departments, organizations, and entities achieve a coordinated response in the face of a large-scale and complex event.

What is the distinct meta-leadership mindset? What is its value during times of crisis? Meta-leadership is the intentional drive to forge both analytic and pragmatic linkages, based on a method of perceiving, understanding, anticipating, and acting. Meta-leaders shape connections among the array of relevant people and interests across the extended enterprise, and do so through leading down, up, and across. These deliberate linkages leverage deductive insights that are applied to the strategic and integrated posture of the meta-leader. Achieving this requires attending to and practicing all the dimensions of meta-leadership simultaneously.

For example, what results from the link between dimension one, the person, and dimension two, the situation? During a crisis, the sensation of panic, the biases, and the personal distortions among some in leadership positions can distract and misdirect the perceptions of the situation. A chasm forms between what is actually happening and what leaders perceive to be happening, a phenomenon that can take the response astray. The discipline and balance that constitute the first dimension of meta-leadership practice direct the leader toward accurate analysis of the circumstances surrounding the event, a purposeful link intended to drive optimal situational awareness.

Similarly, when dimension three, leading down, is combined with dimension four, leading up, organizational vertical connectivity is enhanced, increasing the likelihood that strategies from higher levels translate effectively into operations and tactics at the lower levels and that information, problems, and successes at the front lines provide essential feedback to the top. This ensures that situational awareness at all levels of the organization then translates into effective refinement of strategies and operations. And when these four dimensions are linked with dimension five, leading across, then other organizations, agencies, and individuals that constitute the extended disaster response enterprise are included in a wider scope of awareness and functions. Deliberately paying attention and then intentionally linking these five dimensions of practice is what drives the practice of meta-leadership.

Admiral Allen's Experience

On April 20, 2010, the Deepwater Horizon mobile drilling unit suffered a catastrophic explosion and fire that engulfed the rig. While 111 of the crew on board were saved, 11 died. On April 22, the rig sank in over 5,000 feet water in the Gulf of Mexico, precipitating the largest maritime oil spill in U.S. history—truly a "wicked problem" of the first order.

The response to the Gulf oil spill provides unique insights into the application of the principles of meta-leadership in one of the largest crises encountered by the United States in recent history. From April 20 to May 1, the response was managed regionally under the supervision of Rear Admiral Mary Landry, the Coast Guard commander for the Gulf region. As the gravity of the situation revealed itself and the prospect of the spill affecting all five

Gulf states loomed, a spill of national significance was declared, and I was assigned as the national incident commander on May 1. The well was capped on July 15 and then permanently killed on September 19, ending the source of the spill. Residual cleanup activities still continue as of this writing and a Natural Resource Damage Assessment is in progress.

The concept of a spill of national significance and the role of a national incident commander were created in law and regulation in the Oil Pollution Act of 1990, following the Exxon Valdez spill in 1989. The act created a national level command to ensure a whole of government (that is, enterprise) response and to deal with the complex crosscutting issues that surfaced in the Exxon Valdez case. This included a provision for the government to designate a responsible party (RP) and hold that party accountable for all costs associated with the response and restoration of the environment. It recognized that the private sector was responsible for coordinating and paying for the response under the oversight and direction of the federal government through the Federal On-Scene Coordinator, who is a Coast Guard or Environmental Protection Agency official vested with the authority to direct the RP to action. Failure to respond to the direction of the Federal On-Scene Coordinator exposes the RP to both civil and criminal sanctions.

Oil and hazardous materials spills fall under federal jurisdiction, unlike natural disasters, which are the prime responsibility of state and local governments that can, if they so desire, request federal assistance. This is an extraordinarily important facet to understanding the event and the interrelationships between the dimensions of meta-leadership practice. Having served as the principal federal official for the response to hurricanes Katrina and Rita in the same region, I observed that the legal authorities involved in the spill and the existence of an RP—as opposed to an act of nature— created a much different and in many ways more challenging enterprise context. Because of this, the Gulf spill offers a unique lens through which to view the interrelationship and interaction of the five dimensions of meta-leadership practice.

A comprehensive review of the Gulf spill is well beyond the scope of this article, and it is not my intent to provide an exhaustive retrospective of the event. That said, this is a singular event in the history of the United States, one that clearly frames the dimensions of meta-leadership and their interactions when applied in practice.

Dimension One: The Person of the Meta-Leader

The first dimension of meta-leadership concerns the personal factors that encourage or inhibit effective leadership during a crisis, including emotional factors, along with systematic methods to manage them. With so much at stake during a crisis, involuntary emotional responses are triggered by what is unfolding. This includes fear, not only for what is happening in the moment but also for what could result. Typically in a crisis situation, thinking descends to primal level, hindbrain function—the "basement." To ascend up and out of the basement, routine procedures and protocols—the "toolbox"—are activated to reset clearer, steadier thinking and action. Once emotional stability is reestablished, higher-level, prefrontal cortex strategic thinking and guidance can be achieved. This process occurs in a disciplined, stepwise fashion. One cannot go from the basement to higher-level thinking without first using the toolbox.

The meta-leader recognizes that he or she serves as a role model for followers who observe and then mimic his or her behavior. When the leader is composed and self-assured, others are more likely to be calm and focused. When the leader displays panic, it frightens others and thereby amplifies the collective sense of alarm, further complicating the rallying of a meaningfully helpful response to the crisis. The emotional intelligence at the foundation of meta-leadership practice drives the self-awareness, self-regulation, empathy, motivation, and social skills that unleash the capability to deal effectively with crises. The intent is to optimally perceive and understand what is happening in order to clearly galvanize the other dimensions of meta-leadership practice.

Admiral Allen's Experience

Meta-leaders must—among many things—first know themselves, their emotional flash points and the limits of their own knowledge. Also, they must know how to seek counsel and provide counsel. Ultimately, they must be able to apply their emotional intelligence to create a shared vision that drives enterprise-wide unity of effort. How is this accomplished? The meta-leader focuses on the event and the solutions demanded of the situation as his or her sole purpose. It requires the ability to create a state of mind that is independent from, yet cognizant of, competing interests. These include political views, the emotion and pathos of the event, and the amplification of information by the media, all of which can easily become distractions. The meta-leader, however, finds a way to rise (metaphorically) above the immediacy of the crisis. This demands maintaining a view of what is happening through the lens of an enterprise-wide, even whole of community, response and the national interest, without losing one's grasp on the details and demands of the present. I found that during both the hurricane and spill responses, there was a thirst for a single, credible face and voice to speak to the American public that reflected these aspects of the meta-leader. I had to acquire the public's confidence. The first step in gaining public trust involved communicating to the public that my sole responsibility was to the successful response that was required. The message could not be attenuated or altered by political views. Others have that job by virtue of their positions.

The second step is the clear, unambiguous explanation of what is occurring in a way that increases public understanding of the complexity of the event and the challenges associated with solving the problem. This sometimes entails rapid learning that demands the quick assimilation of new knowledge. During the Gulf spill, I had to immerse myself in engineering concepts associated with deep water drilling. Likewise, during the hurricane response, I had to quickly gain a grasp of the technical issues associated with levee construction and flood plain mapping. Since the meta-leader cannot anticipate the type or level of complexity of the event, preparation requires a commitment to lifelong learning. It has been said, and I believe it, that great leaders are great learners.

Ultimately, a meta-leader must recognize when the event demands that he or she act to inspire a wide audience of responders, leaders, and other stakeholders across the extended enterprise and the nation itself. The challenge rests in understanding that when the stakes are highest, the leader's impact is greatest. It is when we are at most risk personally that our behaviors define us. It is in these circumstances that meta-leaders find that they must maintain their own morale and act to raise the morale of others.

During the oil spill and hurricane responses, I encountered repeated cases where individuals had been demoralized by long work hours, intense media criticism of the response, and lack of recognition for their personal sacrifices. Because of this, when I spoke to the nation, I spoke to the responders from the various components of the enterprise as well, to ensure that they could see themselves in the narrative that explained the responses. The nation demands this kind of leadership, but in truth, the success of the response hangs on whether the responders know it and believe it as well.

Dimension Two: The Situation

Even beyond self-awareness, the meta-leader actively pursues situational understanding and anticipation: these are essential for aligning those under the meta-leader's direct supervision or command, as well as to influence others outside that direct line of authority across the enterprise. Leading up to one's superiors, especially when they are elected or politically appointed officials, presents its own complexities, as larger political and organizational factors must be understood and accounted for. And certainly, the potential for leveraging cross-silo and cross-sector connectivity of action requires the meta-leader to recognize the complementary capabilities and resources that could derive from joint engagement.

There are natural and predictable inclinations among people involved in a crisis that the meta-leader is instructed to expect and then surmount. This is not easy. In a crisis, gut survival instincts have significant bearing on thinking and behavior, potentially overwhelming higher-order strategic judgment. Lingering rivalries and antagonisms can rise to the fore, straining relations among stakeholders just when they are most needed. Often, one situation impacts many different constituencies in unique ways. Each constituency perceives a unique set of risks to what they value. There could be life and death risk, business risk, political risk, and reputational risk, to name but a few. Though these may ultimately be of lower priority and may constitute a distraction, the meta-leader cannot assume that these secondary factors can be ignored. They contribute to that larger dynamic that the meta-leader must calibrate and balance. The meta-leadership model directs deliberate attention to these obstacles and provides flexible methods to transcend them and forge the very relationships and linkages that must be leveraged in times of crisis. Often, this connectivity of effort is a function of the influence, well beyond assigned authority, that the meta-leader has cultivated and is able to exercise.

Admiral Allen's Experience

The meta-leader must have as clear a grasp of the event or situation and the associated context as is possible under the circumstances. While that context will vary according to the specific circumstances associated with the event, several basic concepts are key to defining the problem correctly. First, to the extent that there are legal authorities and jurisdictions involved, they need to be clearly understood. In many cases there will be overlapping jurisdictions, roles, and responsibilities. It is important to understand but not become completely captive to the legal framework. It is a starting point to assess the event and the boundaries of the participating entities and individuals. A pragmatic, seasoned counsel who comprehends the role of advising versus dictating terms is important to formulating the art of the possible.

The Deepwater Horizon drilling unit was located forty-five miles off the Louisiana coast, outside state jurisdiction. The response to this spill was governed by federal law. Unlike a natural disaster where state and local governments have primary responsibility, oil spill responses preempt local jurisdictions, creating dynamic tension among local leaders who want to be seen as relevant and consequential in the response. In this case, as the national incident commander, I had to balance the impulses of local leaders with the considerations of a large-scale disaster. Adding to the political complications, the president was a Democrat, the spill occurred just before midterm congressional elections, and all five Gulf states affected were led by Republican governors.

Second, events that require meta-leaders are complex by nature. Being able to limit that complexity and create a framework to understand the event is critical. This includes challenging assumptions, creating analogies to other events or experiences, and building new assumptions when needed, employing systems thinking and mental models. The meta-leader must envision the event as a system or network, not as an isolated event.

I considered the Gulf spill as a system of events happening within a complex ecosystem rather than as a single event. The first priority was capping the well and eliminating the discharge. The next priority was to recover or mitigate the impact of oil at sea near the wellhead before it could threaten land. After that, strategies were required to keep the oil offshore if possible and then, finally, to remove oil that reached the shore. Each phase required distinct operational responses, competencies, and capabilities to be applied simultaneously in widespread physical and geographic regions.

Dimension Three: Leading Down

The bulk of the literature on leadership addresses meta-leadership dimension three, leading down to direct reports and subordinates. Themes across this wide literature focus on enhancing performance, developing vision and execution, as well as improving system efficiencies and effectiveness. Leading down is about being boss to people who work under the direction, authority, and supervision of the person or people in charge.

In leading down, meta-leaders encourage and enable subordinates to recognize and appreciate that their work and endeavors are actually part of a much larger whole. Because the meta-leader perceives that whole and why it matters, he or she is able to communicate and animate the picture, bringing it to life in a way that is motivating and engaging. The role and responsibility of the boss is to select the right people for the job and create the conditions by which these subordinates can succeed.

What does this wide-angle perspective add to the day-to-day activities of these bosses and their followers? If followers see and understand the big picture clearly, it imbues with them a sense of meaning and purpose. Their work has significance, and they feel a sense of drive. This is the valuable mindset that meta-leaders instill. They recognize, convey, and galvanize this motivating awareness. For followers, the meta-leader's perspective inspires their work and productivity. How is this accomplished? Meta-leaders are active learners and teachers; they are genuinely curious about the people who work under their command and willing teachers through what they do, say, and role-model.

Admiral Allen's Experience

I have been exposed to a lot of thinking, writing, and discussion on leadership that focuses on the role of the leader in dealing with subordinates, that is, leading down. Meta-leadership requires many of the same skills but applied in unique circumstances on a larger scale. Chief among these skills is the ability to simply communicate the values associated with the effort under way that can underscore a single vision and unity of effort.

Meta-leaders must be able to galvanize all their "troops" (whether they officially report to the leader or not) and create a cause for action under the most difficult circumstances. After arriving in New Orleans on September 5, 2005, and working to reset the response and create unity of effort, I was asked to take over direction for the entire Gulf response four days later. As I walked through the Federal Emergency Management Agency (FEMA) Joint Field Office in Baton Rouge before the press conference with Department of Homeland Security Secretary Mike Chertoff, I stopped to talk with a FEMA worker about her experience. In tears she told me how hard she had been working since her arrival and how hard it was to see her organization and leaders vilified in the media. She said, "I go back to my hotel room at night after working twenty straight hours and can't turn on the television." Those words hit me like a bolt of lightning.

After a very painful press conference where Secretary Chertoff announced that I would replace Mike Brown as the principal federal official, I walked back to my new office and pondered my challenge and the words of the FEMA employee. When asked by my executive assistant what I was going to do, I said, "I want to meet with everyone in this building." This was not easily done. The Joint Field Office covered three square blocks where an old Dillard's store and warehouse once operated, and there were over 5,000 people working there. When my assistant told me it was impossible to talk to all of them at once, I said, "Get as many as you can in one place; the word will spread."

Thirty minutes later I stood before nearly 2,000 people in what used to be the first floor of that Dillard's store. I climbed up on a desk with a loud-hailer. After explaining how I would transition from New Orleans to this new role, I said this to the crowd, "I am giving you an order. You are to treat everyone you come in contact with that has been affected by this storm as if they were your own family . . . your mother, father, sister, brother, grandmother. I am telling you this for two reasons. First, if you err, you will err on the side of doing too much, and that is OK. Second, if someone has a problem with what you are doing, you tell them to see me because I gave the order."

In truth, I did not have any authority to order anybody. That said, the situation dictated that someone speak to the thousands of people who were critical to the response and who had been disenfranchised and demoralized. In fact, people began to openly weep, and there was a collective sigh that changed the barometric pressure in the room. No one had ever told these people that their work was important. No one shared or inspired them with the values that formed the vision for the response. More importantly, no one had told them that someone, even metaphorically, had their backs. Things went better from that time forward.

Dimension Four: Leading Up

Everyone who works in a large organization has a boss. Middle managers have bosses who have their own boss, and top bosses have constituents to whom they are accountable: a board of directors, a customer base, or an electorate. Those who work in matrixed organizations may have multiple bosses. Because of the complexity of crisis situations, with so much at stake for so many different constituencies, crisis leaders often are leading up to many bosses, each of whom may have different criteria for success.

How does one chart the course for leading up? Just as curiosity applies to learning and teaching subordinates, these same qualities assist in leading up. The job is to help the boss make good decisions; part of the task is finding how that is best accomplished for a specific boss and then delivering on what is learned. Priorities, decisions, and actions are balanced through intentional communication and education, calculating the power-authority equation between boss and subordinate: in what decisions and actions does the boss want involvement and in which is independence expected? And when it is believed that the boss is miscalculating or misbehaving in fulfilling roles and responsibilities, it may require delivering "truth to power," the most difficult aspect of leading up.

Admiral Allen's Experience

There is a natural gap that arises between career government workers, technical experts, public safety officials, and the academic community and political leaders. That gap is created by the differing roles, expectations, and constituencies of each group. While leading up can take on a variety of meanings, in the context of meta-leadership, I believe it is the ability of the meta-leader to understand the natural vertical separations that occur in governments and organizations and to bridge those gaps.

In the case of the Gulf oil spill, there were extensive gaps between the knowledge of senior political leaders at all levels of government and the detailed expertise that was being used to address the problem. From the technical complexities of deep water drilling and oil production to response techniques that included the use of dispersants and in situ oil burning, there was a constant need to communicate the technical challenges that had to be overcome and to ensure the informed consent of leaders to the actions that were taking place.

One of the most serious threats to a crisis response is the need of other leaders to be relevant in a crisis (and their ability to act on it). A response that appears too technical for them to understand or explain to their constituents can generate the urge for them to act independently, putting the response and their credibility at risk. During both the hurricane and oil spill responses, I had many occasions to interact with and brief two presidents. Regardless of political affiliation, elected leaders want to be informed and consequential in the decisionmaking for which they are accountable to the public.

In the case of the oil spill, key decisions revolved around understanding the forces acting on the damaged well, which was one mile below the surface where there was no human access. Nonetheless, the most important decisions surrounding the capping of the well were based on briefings to the president that allowed him to understand the complexity of the situation and the risks involved. The decision to cap the well carried a risk that pressure in the well could result in damage to the well bore, with large quantities of oil seeping into the nearby formations and flowing to the sea floor where there would be no way to stop it.

This was the most careful and deliberate part of the response, and it required extra communication time to make sure that our leaders gave informed consent and understood the risk. In this instance, the well was capped and there was no leak. I received criticism for allowing additional time for this process to occur, but it was time well spent—leading up.

Dimension Five: Leading Across

The fifth dimension of meta-leadership practice is about leading across: building connectivity of effort among different silos of activity or expertise across the extended enterprise. While the meta-leader bears authority within his or her sphere of responsibility, that same directive clout is not present when dealing with other key interagency and intergovernmental actors. Being effective in leading across requires the meta-leader to establish influence well beyond his or her authority. This is established through development of relationships and lines of communication and, with that, the accrual of respect and regard across a wide community of stakeholders.

The meta-leader is followed for his or her integrity, the cause championed, and the belief that he or she will accomplish the mission in the moment. The outcome of this ability to lead across is unity of effort, a critical factor in meta-leading through an expansive and complex crisis. The meta-leader inspires with the capacity to assemble people to solve complex problems and elicits belief in and aspiration for what can be achieved. This is the essence of meta-leadership: the capacity to see above and beyond what is to envision what could be; to design and assemble social endeavors and enterprises that accomplish more because they are able to leverage a wider expanse of human motivation, capability, and investment.

Admiral Allen's Experience

There is no single complex problem or crisis encountered today that can be adequately dealt with by a single person, agency, leader, private sector firm, or volunteer organization. The challenges the country currently faces defy boundaries set by statute, regulation, policy, appropriations, available resources, competency, and capacity. It is a plain truth that coordination, networking, and collaboration are indispensable: the enterprise leader must have the capacity to lead across a range of participating entities. With the exception of military operations carried out under Title 10 of the U.S. Code, there is no monolithic unity of command that ensures unity of effort. In most cases, cross-boundary leadership is based on trust or moral authority. In some cases, true cross-jurisdictional issues arise where several agencies have authority over the same event or jurisdiction. In those cases, roles must be defined and conflicts adjudicated in order to focus energy on the event itself.

The Gulf oil spill entailed numerous boundary issues at the federal, state, and local level that severely tested our ability to create unity of effort. The Coast Guard, the National Oceanic and Atmospheric Administration (NOAA), and the Environmental Protection Agency all had major roles in the response, as defined in law and regulation. NOAA and the Fish and Wildlife Service both had jurisdiction over wildlife. NOAA and the Food and Drug Administration both had roles in seafood testing. The Occupational Health and Safety Administration had a role in workplace safety for responders. While the National Response Team was designated to work out interagency issues associated with the response, it soon became apparent that we were dealing with issues that were not contemplated by the response doctrine. I spent a good deal of time personally briefing the cabinet secretaries that were involved, but

I needed a streamlined way to deal with crosscutting issues in order to arrive at effective solutions quickly.

In the case of the spill response, leadership of the key participating federal agencies created a new entity called the Interagency Solutions Group (IASG). All of the detailed subject matter experts were needed to update information to be delivered to the different departments, but there was no way to organize them collectively to act as a group. To that end, a room was set up and filled with tables and computers, and each department and agency was given a seat and access to all information associated with the response. I started referring complex, cross-boundary questions to them for solutions and found that they self-organized and zealously attacked each task. The Flow Rate Technical Group, a spin-off of the IASG structure, ultimately assumed control and established an independent government position on the estimated amount of oil that was escaping from the well. By the time the response concluded, the IASG had established itself through its performance as the go-to place in the National Incident Command. I recommended it be permanently part of future response organizations.

Advantage of Meta-Leadership

What is the advantage of the meta-leadership model and method for leading through a crisis? It is the awareness and anticipation of divisive factors combined with tools to surmount them. Through observation of numerous leaders and organizations before, during, and after a crisis, we have found that the moment to practice meta-leadership is not once the crisis has begun. Rather, if the principles and practices are applied to everyday leading and functioning, they become readily available when they are needed in times of a major crisis. How can this be accomplished?

In fact, organizations and their leaders experience crises of a minor nature every day: a personnel crisis, budget crisis, or information technology crisis. Likewise, crises are experienced routinely in the lives of relationships and families; for example, there are numerous crisis learning opportunities for parents raising an adolescent to adulthood. The advantage of incorporating meta-leadership principles and practices into one's routine work and life is that they become available when they matter most.

Once meta-leadership has become part of regular organizational functioning, there are numerous strategic benefits derived from the associated precrisis connectivity of effort, both up and down vertically within organizations and horizontally across the enterprise of crisis preparedness and response. This is particularly true for government organizations in times of fiscal austerity, when they are expected to do more with less budget, personnel, and authority. Cross-enterprise linkages established in noncrisis periods can be leveraged during an emergency to promote the sharing of information and resources that enhance situational awareness as well as the coordination of asset deployment. Embedding meta-leadership thinking and practices encourages the very shifts in behavior and relating that fosters those linkages.

How can meta-leadership be embedded into routine organizational operations so that it can be applied during times of crisis? Ultimately, establishing meta-leadership organizational thinking and operations requires a shift in institutional reward structures. In most cases, interagency, intergovernmental, and cross-sector collaborations are not only discouraged but could be seen as disloyal to one's constituency and conspiring with the competition, in particular when organizational cultures are fixated on amassing resources, authority, and competitive advantage. In that atmosphere, to encourage collaboration is to threaten colleagues, who fear losses in the fight to secure funding, power, and dominance. Organizations as well as individuals who demonstrate meta-leadership practices and who are able to document its benefits deserve the recognition and reward for turning collaboration itself into an operational asset.

PART II

What Makes for an Effective Enterprise Leader?

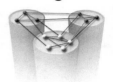

5

Leading the Enterprise through Network Governance

JACKSON NICKERSON

Rick Thomas was in his fifties and a GS-15 working for the Department of Defense's Test Resource Management Center when one of the great challenges of his career was foisted upon him: he was asked to improve the management of U.S. missile ranges. His charge was to increase operational effectiveness while lowering cost, but the odds of success were not good. A 1989 congressional study indicated that low operational performance and excessive costs plagued the missile launch ranges. Indeed, the Test Resource Management Center was created in part to improve performance and reduce cost. More recent studies, however, indicated that little progress had been made because the same issues persisted. For several years, Rick's predecessor worked on these issues but to no avail. Now it was Rick's turn to tackle the impossible.

The core of the challenge was that thirty-three different government agencies had a role and interest in the missile ranges. For instance, the Air Force, National Aeronautics and Space Administration, National Security Agency, and many other agencies use various communications hardware and other equipment located on the ranges. Making any progress in improving performance and reducing costs required most (if not all) of these agencies—especially the

Air Force, as it controls the principal operating budget for the missile ranges—to accept and be willing to implement the steps to be taken.

Leading the enterprise to coordinate and collaborate across this network of agencies with interconnected responsibilities but competing and unaligned interests was a complex and unstructured—some might call wicked—challenge. But this sort of challenge is not unique. A case can be made that since 9-11 the U.S. government has faced, with increasing frequency, wicked problems that can only be effectively handled by interorganizational collaboration and action. Hurricane Katrina, the Deepwater Horizon oil spill, terrorism, the Haiti earthquake, ending homelessness for veterans, and many other wicked problems cannot be solved by one agency or at times even one government.

To make progress in responding to and resolving wicked problems that span the government enterprise, collaboration and coordination within and across federal agencies, between federal agencies and nongovernmental organizations, between military and nonmilitary organizations, and among governments is needed. In sum, responding to wicked challenges requires a "network" of organizations with the collective authorities, resources, and capabilities to jointly tackle the problems. If this idea sounds difficult, it is! How can leaders increase the likelihood of solving wicked problems through networks?

The Promise and Pain of Relying on Networks

For the purpose of this chapter, a network refers to a group of actors that have the potential (which may or may not be realized) to collaborate and coordinate to undertake collective action to achieve some purpose—in our case, solving wicked problems that span the enterprise. The defining feature of a network is that it lacks a central, decisionmaking authority with the right to control and direct the actions of all the network participants; otherwise, the group of actors is no more than a hierarchy. In other words, the key attribute of a network is that participants voluntarily choose to collaborate and coordinate. Under this definition, a network could comprise any number and type of actors, whether they come from a variety of organizations or are all located within the same organization (as long as senior managers are not involved in controlling and directing activities).

Leading networks to tackle wicked challenges through coordination and collaboration is a growing and vital challenge for government leaders. This need for leadership across a network is amplified by the current and potentially long-term era of austerity in which the nation and government leaders now find themselves. Government leaders not only need to find ways to do the same with less—potentially much less—they need to find ways to do *more* with much less, especially when addressing the growing number of wicked issues that span the enterprise.

Leading networks to address and resolve wicked problems has the potential to capture great efficiencies if agencies can rely on other organizations instead of vertical integration, which is costly and often leads to substantial redundancies across agencies. In addition, faster responses may be feasible if organizations draw on others' existing resources and capabilities instead of building their own or relying on the bureaucracy of their own large organizations.

While networks may hold the promise of more efficient, flexible, and rapid responses to wicked challenges, there is no guarantee that networks will actually succeed. Indeed, coordination and collaboration are no easy feat. Networks can be fragile: disrespect, envy, anger, and fear create conflicts that quickly shatter voluntary collaboration, which creates the need for more costly and formal organization and control mechanisms through hierarchies.

FIGURE 5-1. Revenue Growth from Alliances, Fortune 1000 Corporations

Percent

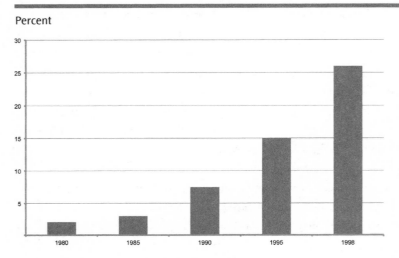

Sources: Columbia University, European Trade Commission, Studies by Booz Allen Hamilton, Anderson Consulting, 1983–87, 1988–93, 1994–96, 1999.

The good news is that if the recent trends in the private sector are any guide, there is cause for hope. The incidence of nonhierarchical collaboration among organizations has exploded in the past few decades. Consider the revenue growth among Fortune 1000 firms that derives from interfirm collaboration. As shown in figure 5-1, the data prior to 1990 support the claim that most firms suffered from a not-invented-here syndrome that discouraged collaboration. But due to a wide variety of factors, post-1990 collaboration grew to represent a substantial portion of firm revenue. To be clear, jointly producing revenue involves a variety of contractual commitments and obligations, which in many ways makes the private sector model of collaboration and coordination unsuitable for the government to emulate. Nonetheless, the fact that a substantial cultural shift took place in the private sector bodes well for a similar cultural shift among government sectors and nongovernmental organizations.

Prerequisites for Leading the Enterprise: Network Governance

Collaboration and cooperation across the enterprise do not occur spontaneously nor are they cost free. Instead, government leaders must build, maintain, and, in some instances, repair networks if they are to be effective in solving wicked problems. This chapter advocates a specific approach for leading networks called "network governance." The premise is that adopting the four practically oriented components of network governance can increase greatly the likelihood of leading networks to solve wicked problems. The four components are common communication codes and channels, trust and reputation, dependence balancing, and mutual incentives. Those government leaders who successfully incorporate these four components within a network create the necessary and sufficient conditions for networks to succeed.

To be candid, while these four components may sound useful, there remains the core leadership question: "What do I have to do to build these components of network governance?" My view is that adopting and following some very specific processes can generate common communication codes, build reputation and trust, balance dependence, and shape mutual incentives all at the same time. Doing so provides the foundation for governing the network that enables the enterprise leader to resolve conflicts or avoid them in the first place and to work toward a common objective. Indeed, after briefly describing each of the four components and what they mean, we will return to Rick's story to explore one such process he adopted for leading.

Communication

Without effective communication, networks can disintegrate rapidly or fail to form in the first place. Good communication hinges on two criteria: it has to be low cost, and people have to understand what is said. Both criteria can be difficult to meet. Communication cost is often considered from a technological perspective, but the real cost of communication is the willingness to listen to one another. Positive social ties—friendships, or at least mutual respect—are the foundation of low-cost communication. No high-speed communications system can overcome unwillingness to listen. The vital and necessary conditions for low-cost communication arise from cultivating social connections and relationships—something many people refer to as building a social network. With respect to a network tasked with solving a wicked problem, it is important to build social relationships not only with all the key leaders but also at multiple touch points up and down the organizations in the network to create redundancy. Relying on only a single network connection point for your organization creates a fragility that can dissolve your organization's connection should the key leader behave in a way that undermines trust and reputation, which is described below. Given the frequent turnover rate due to the career paths of political appointees, civil servants, and military personnel, such redundancy is crucial for network survival.

With the willingness to listen as one criterion, the ability to understand each other is the second. Organizations, professions, and even many families have their own special language to ease communication costs. The specialized language that lowers communication costs within a group raises costs between groups. For instance, it is not uncommon for organizations to have different meanings for the same words and acronyms or use different words and acronyms that have the same meaning. In substantial as well as nuanced ways, if network members do not invest in common language and protocols, conflict will emerge far more easily than understanding.

Trust and Reputation

Entwined with the building of a network are the intangible elements of trust and reputation. A common expression in management is that one cannot manage that which is not measured. Though trust and reputation are not readily measured, they are nonetheless necessary for leading networks. Trust emerges as network members display good character, good will, and good ability. Good character comes from the integrity of being true to one's word. Good will means caring about others and acting to support them, even when it may be costly to the individual. Good ability comes from demonstrating one's capability to achieve successful outcomes. A network not only relies on actors to display these qualities but also provides the channels that communicate trust and reputation, whether negative or positive.

In forming a network, trust and reputation are central, and therefore the network is particularly fragile and sensitive to lack of judgment, faulty perceptions, and poor communication. Thus particular care is needed during network formation, as well as at other times, when new network members join, or else poor judgment, mistakes, or mischaracterizations can create reservations that foreclose, at least in the short term, the possibility of using network governance.

Dependence Balancing

The asymmetry that occurs when one organization bears more risk than another naturally creates concerns that can destabilize a network. This possibility is especially relevant when trying to resolve high-stakes, wicked problems. It is all too easy for rumor and innuendo to slither through a network, opening cracks and undermining trust and understanding. Maintaining a balance so that each network member has something of similar magnitude to gain and lose can fill the cracks and make network ties resistant to such disintegration. Examples of dependency balancing include requiring network members to concurrently invest similar levels of resources and manpower in the problem as well as ensuring that all reputations will be equally exposed should the network not advance toward a solution.

Mutual Incentives

Common goals and desires create a foundational incentive for common action. It is not unusual that early on, network members do not fully perceive and appreciate that they have mutual incentives. Yet, if there is a willingness to listen and understand, mutual incentives might be found. Alternatively, through the process of working together and engagement, network members can find, shape, and build mutually shared incentives. For instance, it is not unusual for actors to identify mutual incentives once they share experiences or work together in figuring out a problem. In essence, they become engaged as a team and support each other much like a cohesive military unit.

Implementing Network Governance: An Example

Network governance requires leaders, individually and collectively, to build, maintain, and, in some instances, repair networks to effectively lead a collaborative effort to solve wicked problems.

Leadership by government executives is essential to creating the components of network governance. Network leadership requires ongoing attention to communication, trust and reputation, dependence balancing, and mutual incentives. Those government leaders who successfully establish these four components will provide a great service to our nation because they will lead their network to solve wicked problems relatively quickly and efficiently. Rick Thomas provides one such example.

Rick did bring together all thirty-three agencies to discuss the issue. Lacking direct authority over any of the participants, he utilized a particular process called collaborative structured inquiry (CSI). CSI is just one process that offers several unique features with which to build the four components of network governance. For example, while typical meetings frequently allow participants to jump to conclusion and solutions, which stoke competition, conflict, and crisis, CSI uses facilitation to focus on first discussing only the symptoms of the issue. The facilitator uses a round-robin arrangement to ask participants to share only one symptom or indicator of the problem from their perspective. Doing so avoids domination of the meeting by one or a few individuals and ensures participation of those who might otherwise remain quiet or acquiesce.

This first phase helps increase listening and builds trust. It enables groups to figure out language differences, and share information and knowledge using a common language. Ultimately, the group must come to a complete consensus on all of the symptoms. This, in essence, gives everyone a veto, which creates mutual dependence and further builds trust. Once consensus is reached on the symptoms, participants typically begin to "own" the constellation of symptoms, creating mutual incentives. Finally, consensus must be reached on a document and its language to share with the constituencies not at the meeting, a process that enables feedback and verification, which further advances all four components of network governance.

Once this first phase is complete, a second phase is initiated to discover all the root causes. The basic round-robin format is repeated, further enhancing communication, trust and reputation, dependence balancing, and mutual incentives across the entire network. When consensus again is reached and a document is sent out to the constituencies for verification, not only is the wicked problem fully formulated in terms of symptoms and causes, but also the entire network (now a team) typically takes ownership of the problem and finds a solution all can agree with. This agreement naturally leads to rapid implementation.

Rick facilitated the CSI process. In truth, processes to create network governance take a lot of time, especially at the beginning— how else can one encourage communication, build trust and reputation, balance dependence, and create mutual incentives? But the payoff is that the network can then tackle and solve wicked problems and implement solutions. Rick's facilitation of CSI took ten months—a long time—but all thirty-three agencies did agree on a full set of symptoms, a set of causes, produced a solution everyone agreed to, and began implementation. The group's estimates indicate that the solution saved the citizens of the United States $3 billion and enhanced missile range performance. Rick's leadership led the network to solve its wicked problem.

Success in leading the enterprise can be achieved by developing people so that they possess the competencies and learn the processes to build, maintain, and repair network governance. It is important to acknowledge that leading a network takes a lot of work. Networks can be fragile. Turnover of key network "nodes" can undermine the network and its effectiveness if not managed well. Indeed, with typical two-year political appointments, frequent rotation of military and some civil service personnel, and changes in the White House every four years, maintaining and repairing networks requires frequent, if not near constant, attention in a government setting. Yet the promise of being able to tackle wicked problems that span the enterprise with flexibility and speed and at low cost in a era of fiscal austerity makes leading change through network governance too attractive and too important to ignore.

6

Critical Connections: Driving Rapid Innovation with a Network Perspective

ROB CROSS, ANDREW HARGADON,
AND SALVATORE PARISE

I n recent years, it has become clear to governmental agencies that innovation is essential to improving their ability to adapt quickly to increasingly complex problems. Solving these problems requires that leaders bring together a depth and breadth of expertise—from both inside and outside federal agencies. Yet rather than facilitate fluid collaboration throughout an agency, most efforts to drive innovation stem from the myth of the single, blinding insight. The idea of a brilliant employee or sequestered working group creating the next panacea remains the dream of many agencies as well as private sector organizations. We are seduced by the simplicity of this notion when, in fact, it is usually wrong. For example, the story of 3M's Post-it notes is a story of collaboration and evolution that unfolded between the research scientist, Spencer Silver, and product developer Art Fry and countless others who lent critical support throughout its development. Even Thomas Edison's success depended upon a team of others—from the fifteen engineers in his Menlo Park laboratory to financier J. P. Morgan (and his critical influence over the gas industry and regulatory agencies) to the men like Samuel Insull who grew the utilities that made electricity a profitable business.

We must acknowledge the historical and collaborative roots of most successful innovations and create policies and government entities that enable federal employees to more seamlessly leverage colleagues' expertise at the point of need. This does not mean simply adding more meetings, layering on another collaborative technology, hoping for innovation to occur after a restructuring, or sticking to innovation policy through a "top-down" approach. These solutions present little if any evidence that they are creating connections with a payoff. History teaches us that most breakthrough innovations are recombinations of existing ideas or technologies, the integration of which occurs through informal networks.[1] While traditionally these networks have formed in very serendipitous ways, it is becoming increasingly important for leaders to cultivate and "manage" lateral and external connections. Successful innovation will come from targeted initiatives ensuring connectivity among those with the right expertise in a given domain and those with the right influence—the people who have a unique ability to get things done by virtue of their position in the network.

Failures to innovate effectively and efficiently can often be traced back to two categories of network problems. First is the inability *to effectively recognize, recombine, and leverage expertise that is in-house or accessible through extended networks.* Too often leadership focuses innovation resources in one small group, tells them to scan the horizon for the next breakthrough idea, and ends up missing myriad opportunities to recombine the existing ideas and expertise spread across people within their own organizations or the federal government as a whole. Second is the inability *to react effectively when people do recognize new opportunities.* While the first is a failure to exploit existing expertise and networks at an agency's disposal, the second is an inability to drive change through those networks—to reshape them in ways that create new value and recognize opportunities. This chapter shows how a network perspective can reveal hidden barriers to innovation as well as ways that government agencies can create more vibrant networks.

A Relational View of Innovation

New opportunities become visible if one's perspective shifts to view innovation not as the generation of new ideas by individuals and small groups but rather as the flow of knowledge and capabilities into and across an organization or enterprise. Rather than hiring brilliant individuals, sequestering small teams with a charge to generate a blinding insight, or engaging in yet another organizational restructuring to break down silos, the most valuable approach is mobilizing a network of relevant expertise and capabilities. Mapping information flow, problem solving, and decisionmaking interactions in agencies or groups can reveal patterns of collaboration that either support or undermine innovation. Across more than twenty organizations we have seen this view help leadership address three key innovation obstacles:

—Fragmentation: Collaboration often breaks down across physical distance, functional lines, technical capabilities, rank, tenure, and occupational subcultures in ways that invisibly undermine strategic innovation efforts.

—Domination: The voices of a few central network members can drown out novel ideas, driving innovation efforts along traditional trajectories.

—Insularity: Inability to recognize and leverage relevant external expertise can yield excessive cost structures and time delays that result in missed opportunities.

Of course, these obstacles are not new, but they are increasingly problematic in an environment where rapid and targeted collaboration is central to innovation. This needs to change. The networks distributed throughout an organization, though seemingly invisible and intractable, are potentially powerful levers to improve both the success and efficiency of innovation efforts. In the remainder of this chapter, we discuss each of the above obstacles, accompanied by a short case example to show how a network perspective can help illuminate these biases. We then conclude with five practices leadership can leverage to develop more vibrant networks.

Fragmentation

Leaders often pursue innovation through efforts to integrate specialized expertise via team and project staffing, methodologies to institutionalize new processes or technology, and internal divisional restructurings.[2] Akin to an x-ray examination, network analysis can enable a leader to look inside an organization and see whether collaborations among those with complementary expertise are occurring in ways that support innovation objectives. Unfortunately, it is very common to see networks fragment precisely where management had been counting on integration, despite having all formal levers pulled to promote collaboration.

Consider the plight of a seasoned partner in a well-known professional services firm who had been tasked with leading a group of fifty experts to develop new service offerings. To create client solutions that generated revenue for the firm as quickly as possible, he merged these experts into three tightly knit groups under his control. Each had specific expertise required to move a service offering from idea inception to commercial viability. However, a year after the restructuring, the innovation process had not improved as much as he had hoped based on service offerings produced and revenue impact.

Network analysis provided the ideal approach to demonstrate how collaboration was occurring within and between relevant functions. In this case, we conducted an assessment of the entire group and then highlighted people in the network by their function

FIGURE 6-1. Integrating Expertise at a Professional Services Organization

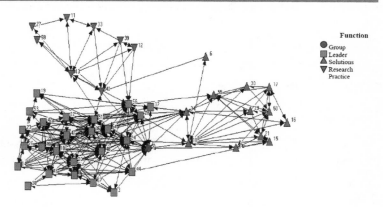

Source: Authors.

to see where lack of integration might be undermining innovation (see figure 6-1).

The information network reveals a lack of integration across functional lines—despite these functions having been merged under one leader—and this fragmentation dramatically undermined innovation. First, there was lack of integration between the research and the solutions groups. The research group was responsible for developing new ideas. The solutions group defined the value proposition, a description of the solution, and created documentation to be used by the firm's consultants. Rather than engage in idea development and commercialization jointly, these two groups had been working sequentially. This resulted in inefficiencies due to misunderstandings in the handoff of an idea and lack of follow-through because ideas were developed in isolation.

Another silo—between the research and the practice groups—undermined the uptake of new offerings. The practice group interacted directly with the firm's consultants in introducing new solutions and so received feedback that could benefit the research group. Unfortunately, the practice group was twice-removed from research: research passed ideas to solutions, which then interacted with the practice group. According to a research group leader, "Sometimes we are thinking in a vacuum and lose the practicality of an idea. The problem is partners don't always have the time to give us feedback. Practice support could be that feedback loop."

Domination

A second network bias arises when a small number of people (often holding expertise most applicable to *past* issues) become dominant in information and decisionmaking networks.[3] Effective innovation derives from more than just having the best and most relevant individuals making decisions. Leaders must also consider how the influence of those with certain kinds of expertise affects opportunity recognition and action. A network perspective can help determine if old paradigms and solutions are dominating the undertaking while more relevant but emerging expertise has been relegated to a peripheral network position.

An example of domination was seen in the information and decisionmaking networks of the research and development (R&D) function in a well-known consumer products organization. Our analysis revealed how the expertise of those in influential network positions had a pervasive and enduring impact on the entire R&D function. For example, to guard against consumer health risks, R&D management hired scientists with specific microbiology expertise. Over time and through seemingly small interactions, these experts moved into highly central and influential network positions. This subtle and invisible movement created an overly rigid informal screening process of new ideas. Prudent risks could have extended innovations, but novel ideas were labeled off-limits in conversations with the experts well before being elevated to decisionmakers for formal consideration.

FIGURE 6-2. Network Dominance of Expertise in Consumer Product R&D

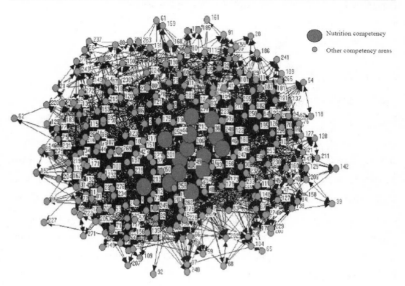

Source: Authors.

Leaders can visualize the comparative influence of expertise by reshaping nodes to reflect each person's knowledge or skills. For example, figure 6-2 shows how one technical competency, nutrition, was central in this R&D network, influencing opportunity recognition in myriad conversations that occurred outside of the formal review process. In this case, senior management indicated that opportunities were being missed because the technical reputation of a few well-connected scientists had become more important than prudent exploration of new and potentially disruptive ideas.

Of course, being an expert is only one determinant of who is heard in an organization. Beyond expertise, dominant voices arise due to power, unique information access, and formal decisionmaking rights. In many cases, leaders strive to remain technical experts or maintain power (as opposed to becoming good leaders) and in the process, drown out alternative perspectives. The more senior the person, the larger this problem can become, as she or he has the ability to drive substantial and possibly off-base investments of funding, employee time, and key resources.

Insularity

For organizations to innovate effectively and efficiently, it is no longer possible to own all competencies and technical expertise. For government agencies specifically, using time more efficiently and reducing costs requires outsourcing innovation efforts (for example, research or development activities) to government contractors. While it is increasingly important for agency leaders to look externally for key knowledge and skills, they must do so with an informed eye to the effectiveness with which critical expertise is sourced and migrates into their organization. A network perspective allows leaders to identify gaps or inefficiencies in sourcing strategies.

Consider a pharmaceutical company that applied network analysis in a number of therapeutic areas to assess the quality of internal and external connectivity. For this company, leveraging research across different medications required effective collaboration both internally among research groups and externally with academic institutions, research centers, and other companies. Figure 6-3 shows the network of a critical therapeutic area, which has an extensive and balanced set of external relationships with academic institutions. Yet even this well-connected therapeutic area caused concern for management due to the concentration of important external relationships among just a few people. Twelve of the organization's scientists held the bulk of important external ties, and the removal of the top four scientists reduced external connectivity by 50 percent (72 out of 143 interactions; see figure 6-4). A very high percentage (80 percent) of the interactions between the pharmaceutical organization and academia were one-on-one, causing

FIGURE 6-3. External Connectivity in Pharmaceutical R&D

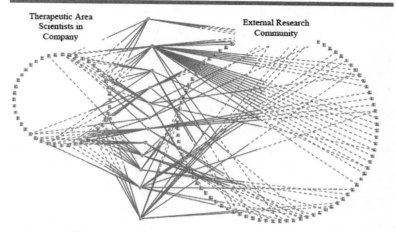

Source: Authors.

FIGURE 6-4. Removal of Top Four Scientists Reduces Connectivity

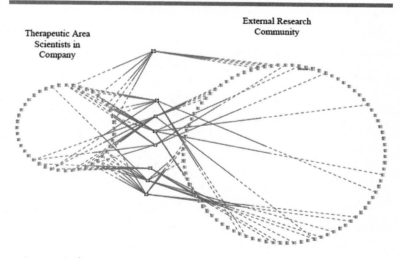

Source: Authors.

management concern about the vulnerability of these critical sources of knowledge should key scientists leave.

These barriers—fragmentation, domination, and insularity—undermine many organizations' abilities to identify and execute innovation opportunities. While examples in the current chapter have been pulled from research done with private sector companies, these barriers are similarly faced by government agencies working to solve complex problems in new and collaborative ways. From a more traditional perspective of innovation as deriving from individual or team achievements, these barriers might be overlooked and considered to have little effect on the quality or speed of the innovation process. But viewing innovation as the flow of knowledge and practice into and across an agency, and the federal enterprise as a whole, reveals how small changes in network characteristics can have large effects. In the following section, we describe five network-centric practices that can be used to overcome network barriers to innovation.

Five Practices to Drive Innovation through Networks

Create a Network-Centric Ability to Sense and Respond to New Opportunities

Innovation often derives from an ability to fluidly capitalize on new opportunities regardless of functional, hierarchical, geographic, or organizational lines. Ideally, networks enable organizations to "surge": to sense opportunities or problems in one pocket of a network and rapidly tap into the expertise of others to coordinate an effective response. This is not about pushing a greater volume of information through a network or fixing current gaps but rather about creating networks that have the ability to accommodate new problems.

Building awareness of who knows what in a network is critical to enable people to tap the right expertise at the right time and thus avoid missed opportunities due to unawareness of existing expertise, as well as incomplete responses due to using only local, less relevant knowledge. Consider an R&D function of a consumer products organization. As part of a broader effort, management held an off-site meeting to help improve collaboration across aspects of formal structure (functional lines, hierarchical levels, project groups). Quite often off-site events serve to entrench networks rather than expand connectivity at points that matter for the organization. To avoid the network trap of staff simply reconnecting with people they already knew, programming was designed to ensure that bridges were built across the gaps that a previous network analysis revealed both existed and had the potential to impede innovation. Everything from how tables were staffed and then rotated to the kinds of problem solving sessions people participated in was geared toward reinforcing connectivity with a potential payoff—not just mingling to build a bigger network.

Develop an Ability to Rapidly Test and Refine an Opportunity and Avoid Gridlock

Effective innovation is about action as much as vision. For the agencies that do this well, executing on innovation is the result of a network that can rapidly combine and deploy resources to test the potential of many different opportunities.

Government organizations need to be able to rapidly explore issues in order to remain agile and collaborate effectively within and across departments, as well as across the federal government as a whole. For organizations that have relied on heavily siloed departments and outdated decisionmaking structures, this represents a fundamental shift away from a single future envisioned by an elite few to rapidly testing a range of possible futures created through more collaborative network relationships. A lack of action often boils down to unclear or overly burdensome decisionmaking processes. When decision rights—who can make what kind of decision—are unclear, everything escalates up the hierarchy, creating bottlenecked networks, slowing the progress of cross-departmental and cross-agency efforts, and sapping the energy of those with innovative insights. Mapping decisionmaking networks can quickly reveal where certain decision rights need to be defined or reallocated to permit more rapid prototyping of ideas. Several high-level leaders have used network analysis to identify people in key network positions and encouraged them to take prudent risks—an approach that helps allay fear and promotes creativity in a targeted and personal way that rapidly diffuses through the network (in contrast to the typical but less effective impersonal exhortations to the masses).

Magnify Returns on Human Capital by Working through Those in Specific Network Positions

People in privileged positions in their organization's information networks—not always those high in the formal hierarchy—can have a substantial impact on how an innovative idea is developed and implemented. Network analysis helps identify individuals in privileged network positions in two ways. First, it identifies key brokers, those who hold the entire network together by virtue of their relationships across subgroups and formal structures. By sitting on the shortest informational path between others in the network, brokers are often the most aware of expertise and resources inside and outside of an organization that can be leveraged. Second, network analysis identifies those with expertise relevant to a given innovation. Creating a network map, coloring nodes (people) in the network by technical competency(-ies), and finding those most sought out for relevant expertise can identify employees with

FIGURE 6-5. Group Managers as Innovation Influencers

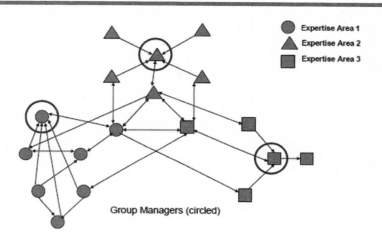

Source: Authors.

both technical depth and ground-level credibility in the eyes of their peers—attributes that are important to both the development and implementation of a new innovation.

Tapping people by virtue of their position in the network increases the likelihood of success by engaging those with the best expertise and greatest influence in the network. This yields a different knowledge and influence base than the more traditional approach where leadership picks either those in positions of formal authority or those they know. Consider figure 6-5, which represents people likely to be selected for an innovation effort based on their formal position. Unfortunately, these people are not the best choices. They are central only in their own group, are most likely to be wedded to a certain way of doing things, may not have a good sense of the capabilities of individuals outside their immediate group, and are not necessarily influential in other groups that might need to coordinate efforts to implement an innovation. In

FIGURE 6-6. Key Brokers as Innovation Influencers

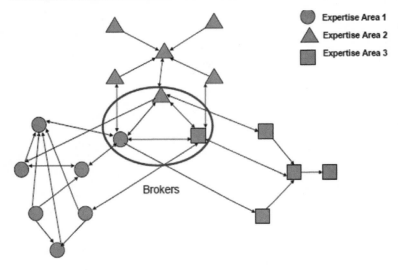

Source: Authors.

contrast, brokers in figure 6-6 are better candidates: their network position makes them more aware of resources and expertise dispersed throughout the organization, and they are more likely to be successful at crafting a viable solution because of their understanding of the political dynamics and cultural values in the subgroups.

Leverage "Energy" in a Network as a
Key Determinant of Innovation and Progress

Up to this point, we have focused on networks solely in terms of information flow. Yet most of us rely on relationships at work for more than just information. In networks where relationships are not prescribed by formal structure, emotion plays a substantial role in determining who people learn from—particularly in creative interactions where someone is on new ground and not just looking for answers to known problems. Mapping energy or enthusiasm in networks—simply asking people to indicate those individuals with whom they leave interactions enthused (versus those that are draining)—provides a powerful indicator of where creativity and innovation is occurring. One executive said, "You have to be energizing to get people to listen to your idea to begin with and certainly energizing to get them to help you implement it or accept it."

Network diagrams of energy or enthusiasm can yield highly revealing results. For example, diagrams can highlight where connectivity is strong across certain areas of expertise such that creativity and effective collaboration is likely to occur. Focusing on these points can be a quick way to gain ground on both planned and emergent innovation opportunities to see where ideas are bubbling up. Similarly, network diagrams help reveal those people who are engaging others in the network. Providing these emergent leaders with room and some resources can leverage the natural flow of ideas in a network. Finally, energy or enthusiasm networks can help a leader locate what we call vacuums (where a lack of energy exists) or vortexes (where negative energy is draining a group) at intersections that must work well for the agency to support the mission.

Network analysis can identify where opportunities for improvement lie, helping leaders target development of specific behaviors that past research has revealed to be consistently associated with positive energy.[4] These behaviors can be developed via coaching, career development processes, embedding behavioral dimensions in project or team evaluations, or simple self-assessment. Regardless of the approach, where energy is lagging, probing on energy issues at either an individual or group level can dramatically improve innovation within an agency or department.

Ensure That Organizational Context Helps
Innovation Occur Fluidly throughout a Network

One of the most common network barriers to an agency's ability to reconfigure resources into innovations stems from the organizational context—formal design, planning and budgeting processes, reward systems, culture, and leadership—that drives parochial behavior. Too heavy a focus on individual achievement or competition between departments or agencies creates silos in networks that undermine innovation opportunities. For example, recently, one top IBM executive publicly criticized the firm's reward structures, which pitted divisions against one another: "We don't talk to people in other operations. They have become the competition. There is no sharing of information and limited cooperation."[5] In our own work, we have seen collaboration between groups stall when it took longer to get approval to "transfer" the human resources from one project to another than to actually get the work done.

While leaders will not be able to entirely overhaul agencies, offices, or divisions to create the ideal collaborative context, they can at least make sure that fragmentation across certain aspects of formal structure is not invisibly impeding innovation. In one company, for example, formal "dual citizenship" roles were established to allow someone in research and development to collaborate with others in the business units without requiring internal budget transfers or formal project reassignments. Another option is to create ad hoc teams around particular organizational capabilities and create a cost structure supporting that team, sharing the burden across more than one business unit. The entire human resources chain can affect collaboration by determining the kinds of people brought into the organization, the way in which they are developed, and the behaviors that are measured and rewarded.

In short, effective collaboration requires a holistic approach. Simply introducing a collaborative technology, tweaking incentives, or advocating cultural programs to promote collaboration is often insufficient. Promoting connectivity requires the alignment of unique aspects of formal organizational design, control systems, technology, and human resource practices. And beyond organizational architecture, specific cultural values and leadership behavior can have a striking effect on patterns of collaboration, often overriding seemingly aligned designs. The right elements of context to work with are unique to each organization. In some settings, battling an entrenched cultural value (a not-invented-here mentality, for instance) can be critical, while in others modifying division-level planning processes and performance metrics is central to improving a network. While it is rarely pragmatic to suggest a total reorientation of organizational design to support a given network, it has been our consistent experience that three to five aspects of context provide high-leverage opportunities for improving collaboration in a way that has a strategic impact for an agency.

Conclusion

In recent years, it has become clear to governmental agencies that innovation is a key component to improving their ability to adapt to internal and private sector demands as well as changing technologies. However, the increased complexity of government challenges, constrained fiscal environment, and new technology have meant that innovation efforts must bring together a depth and breadth of expertise—from within and across government and external organizations—faster and more effectively than ever before. The major barriers to innovation today result not from failures of individual genius but rather from failures of collaboration—

inability to exploit the existing capabilities of an agency in new and revolutionary ways. Here we have identified three of the more common breakdowns in an organization's networks that undermine the innovation process as well as a series of relatively simple but targeted and powerful practices that can help overcome these biases. Effective leaders need to be aware of how skills and abilities are distributed and tapped within the networks that make up their organizations. In today's complex environment, those who can read and harness the networks in and beyond their organizations, quickly diagnose breakdowns in those networks before they become crises, and effectively build new networks around emerging innovations will be the most successful in these increasingly dynamic times.

Notes

1. G. Basalla, *The Evolution of Technology* (New York: Cambridge University Press, 1988); W. E. Bijker, *Of Bicycles, Brakelites, and Bulbs: Toward a Theory of Sociotechnical Change* (MIT Press, 1995); Thomas P. Hughes, *American Genesis: A Century of Invention and Technological Enthusiasm, 1870–1970* (New York: Viking, 1989); F. Kodama, *Emerging Patterns of Innovation: Sources of Japan's Technological Edge* (Harvard Business School Press, 1991).

2. J. S. Brown and P. Hagel, *The Only Sustainable Edge: Why Business Strategy Depends on Productive Friction and Dynamic Specialization* (Harvard Business School Press, 2005); D. Leonard, and W. Swap, *When Sparks Fly: Igniting Creativity in Groups* (Harvard Business School Press, 1999).

3. For some time, scholars have drawn attention to the way in which existing skills and knowledge affect an organization's ability to recognize, assimilate, and take action on key information via such terms as absorptive capacity, competency traps, path dependence, and collective cognition. Network analysis allows a manager to see exactly what knowledge is disproportionately important.

4. R. Cross and A. Parker, *The Hidden Power of Social Networks: Understanding How Work Really Gets Done in Organizations* (Harvard Business School Press, 2004).

5. R. Crow, "Institutionalized Competition and Its Effects on Teamwork," *Journal for Quality and Participation* 18 (June 1995): 47.

7

Leadership in a Networked World: How to Accelerate Organizational Change and Improve Performance

THOMAS W. VALENTE

Many organizations face the challenge of being able to communicate and collaborate across division or agency boundaries. Professionals spend their careers learning the policies, procedures, and culture of one agency, which makes it difficult for them to understand their peers in other agencies. For example, a career FBI officer may find it difficult to understand why CIA officers do some things the way they do. This problem is often referred to as the "silo" problem, a metaphor for the uniqueness and separation of each division within an agency from one another. This chapter approaches leadership from a network perspective to illustrate how the silo problem can impede the flow of information among subgroups. It simulates information diffusion within hypothetical networks based on different initial seed conditions—the originators of the information—and the way subgroups are connected within a broader organization. In essence, it poses the following questions: "What can network analysis offer to help us understand and combat the 'silo' problem," and "How can the network perspective inform ways that directors can accelerate organizational improvement initiatives?"

FIGURE 7-1. Hypothetical Formal Organizational Chart

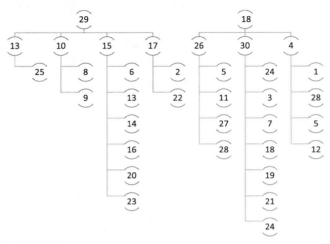

Source: Author.

Formal versus Informal Networks

Organizations have formal hierarchies that set the lines of authority and reporting needed for the organization to function. Figure 7-1 shows a hypothetical formal organizational chart indicating that persons 18 and 29 are directors of two divisions, each with three hierarchical levels: director, manager, and staff. Typically 29 and 18 are considered to have the power to make decisions and delegate tasks to those below them in the hierarchy. Promotion up the hierarchy is valued and is primarily a function of positive evaluations by one's supervisors. There are, however, informal hierarchies and information flows that are often just as important, if not more so, to actual individual and organizational performance.

The numerous informal networks within an organization are composed of the many relationships that exist among organizational members. One informal network, for example, is the set of relations defining who goes to whom for advice about work-related matters. Other organizational relations would be who discusses work-related projects with whom, who is friends with whom, and who goes to lunch with whom. Thus potentially an infinite number of informal networks define intraorganizational relationships, and these networks have important implications for how the organization functions and specific individuals' roles within that operation. For example, an informal network of advice seeking that is sparse, containing few relations, is likely an indication that employees do not know whom to go to for help when they have problems at work. In contrast, a dense informal advice-seeking network, one with many links, indicates that employees have many people to go to for help and thus can effectively problem solve if necessary.

Social network analysis provides a set of tools and techniques useful for analyzing these informal networks and linking them to individual and organizational performance. From a network perspective, one would expect that organizations with dense advice-seeking networks perform better (whatever that may mean) than ones with sparse advice-seeking networks. This is a credible assumption because when employees have many others they can turn to for advice, they can be more productive and not delayed when trying to complete tasks. Other network relationships, such as friendship, trust, or liking, can indicate cohesive organizations—or conversely, fragmented ones.

Leadership from a Network Perspective

Given the distinctions between formal and informal relationships and hence the kind of network structures they generate within organizations, it is clear that network analyses of informal relationships can provide an alternative lens through which to view

FIGURE 7-2. Sample Informal Network: Who Turns to Whom for Advice

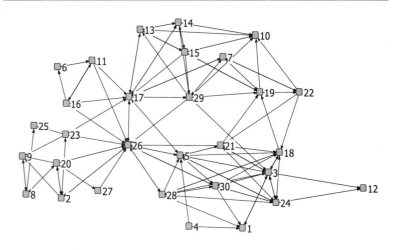

Source: Author.

organizational performance and evolution. Rather than focusing on who reports to whom or who should take orders from whom, the network perspective focuses on who talks to whom and who seeks advice from whom. An alternative view of the organization depicted in figure 7-1 is provided in figure 7-2, which uses hypothetical data to show who turns to whom for advice. The organization now appears to be much less hierarchical, with more and different people occupying critical positions in the network.

Each person in figure 7-2 is labeled with an ID number, and the lines connecting individuals indicate the relationships between people. The arrowheads indicate the direction of the relationship. For example, the link and arrowhead pointing from 22 to 18 indicates that 22 nominated 18 as someone they go to for advice.

The network view of the organization is much different than the formal organization chart in several ways. First, people can have multiple relationships: 22 also has an advice connection with 7, 10, 19, and 21. Second, relationship direction matters quite a bit: some people receive many nominations (for example, 17 and 26) while others receive comparatively few (for example, 4, 6, and 25). There are many tools available to describe and analyze a network like the one shown in figure 7-2, including tools to identify prominent individuals, find subgroups, define equivalent positions, and characterize the network as cohesive or fragmented. For the director of an organization, division, or group, finding important individuals via network analysis can help identify important levers for implementing organizational change programs.[1]

From a network perspective, leaders are those who occupy central positions in a network of relations within an agency or organization. Typically, leaders are defined as having many people who rely on them for advice.[2] The network in figure 7-2, for example has two prominent individuals, 17 and 26, who occupy central positions in the network because many people report 17 and 26 as sources of information, influence, or advice. From a network perspective, leadership is defined as relational rather than dependent on one's role in a formal organizational hierarchy. The network leaders derive their leadership by virtue of other people's reports, not because of their own self-evaluation or status designated by some external authority. It is the wisdom of the crowd that bestows this honor.

Many experimental studies have been conducted using the network approach to identify leaders and recruit them to act as change agents or champions. For example, in two hospitals, Lomas and others contacted physicians who were network opinion leaders and recruited them to promote vaginal birth after the first C-section, a practice supported by federal guidelines.[3] The study showed an 11.9 percent drop in C-sections in those two hospitals during the two-year study whereas the rates increased in the twelve comparison hospitals. In over twenty studies, the opinion leader approach has been shown effective in accelerating practice change.[4]

Leaders identified via network analysis differ from leaders identified with self-report. A recent study compared physicians nominated by their peers as leaders with those individuals self-reporting as leaders using a standardized scale and found little overlap.[5] The correlation between the frequency of being nominated as a leader and physician self-reports was 0.43, which would be described as a modest correlation. Thus, often people think they are leaders when in fact they are not viewed as such by their peers. A second interesting finding of this study was that people who self-identified as leaders were resistant to peer persuasion as an influence on the adoption of new practices whereas leaders identified as such by their peers were open to peer input.

Network analysis therefore can be used to validly and reliably identify organizational leaders and how to engage them in performance improvements. Though leaders are most frequently identified as those receiving the most nominations, other mathematical algorithms can be used to identify individuals located in strategic positions in informal networks, such as those who span disconnected groups (bridges). Such individuals may have few connections, but the ones they have are to well-connected people elsewhere in the network.[6] The following computer simulations demonstrate the utility of using network-identified leaders as change agents.

Simulations

These computer simulations illustrate the role of opinion leaders and informal network structures on organizational performance. Computer simulations provide the opportunity to experiment with different ideas without incurring the cost of actually doing them. Although simulations are limited by what can be envisioned in a computer or mathematical model, and they cannot incorporate the many complexities of real world situations, they can inform our thinking about how to improve organizational performance. As Box and Draper noted, "All models are wrong but some are useful," which definitely applies to simulation models.[7]

The simulations model how fast (or slowly) information can spread or diffuse within an organizational network. Diffusion of innovations and information is important to organizational performance as it describes how new ideas, information, and practices spread and are used by employees.[8] Slow diffusion means delay in the uptake of new processes and may result in catastrophic outcomes for lack of vitally important information. Understanding how to accelerate diffusion and guarantee that critical information and behaviors become widespread in a timely manner can mean the difference between success and failure. These simulations vary two properties: the originators of the information (the seeds), and the overall network structure, that is, whether or not the network is connected, and if disconnected, how to connect it. Thus they model the effects of leadership and boundary spanning, or bridging, simultaneously.

Results

Figure 7-3 indicates the expected benefit derived when information originates with opinion leaders and then spreads to others in the agency. It was generated by creating 100 random networks and comparing how fast information spreads when that information was first learned by members on the margins (periphery), randomly selected members, and opinion leaders. It is clear that when information is first learned by opinion leaders, it spreads much more rapidly than when learned by randomly selected or marginal members. This is important because it indicates that unless leaders are

FIGURE 7-3. Expected Benefit When Information Originates with Opinion Leaders versus Other Pathways

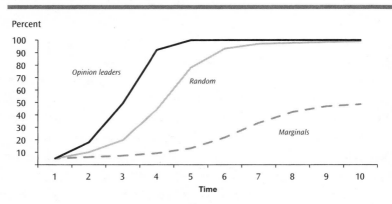

Source: Based on author's calculations.

aware of information early, its diffusion will be delayed considerably. If it is first learned by those on the margins, then its diffusion will be delayed even more and may never reach large segments of the organization.

The trouble is, those on the margins are most often the first to learn of new things. People on the periphery of organizations are often there because they have contacts to people in other agencies or programs. We often think peripheral members are marginal because they are unpopular or just not "people people." While there may be some truth to this, it is not necessarily the case and often stems from people being new to the organization or spending more time with outside entities. For example, an employee tasked with developing a certain program may spend most of his or her time learning that expertise from external agencies or contractors and so have more contacts outside the host organization. Thus an FBI agent charged with monitoring social media activity may spend a lot of time learning from Facebook experts and so have more ties to the private social media industry.

Persons 12 and 4 in figure 7-2, for example, are marginal in the within-division network. The human tendency is to ignore these individuals and treat them as unimportant to agency operation. Yet they provide a very important function because they link to other agencies and organizations. It is difficult for directors to appreciate members on the periphery because they are often literally and figuratively out of sight. This issue can become even more pronounced when considering the "silo" problem.

Many managers are asked to "share" their personnel with other departments or agencies so there can be cross-fertilization. This personnel sharing is often done so that agencies can learn from one another and understand how different divisions within one agency function. The idea is to connect formerly isolated subgroups to enhance the flow of information, with all the benefits that entails.

Figure 7-4 illustrates two of the many ways disconnected divisions can be joined. Link A connects nodes 7 and 19, two nodes that occupy somewhat peripheral positions in their respective subgroups. This is the type of link most often formed between subgroups as these peripheral people are the ones most likely to be connected to other groups. Indeed, it is usually such peripheral people that agency directors are most willing to send on transfer assignments because they are less critical to the division's overall functioning. Link B, in contrast, connects the central individuals from each subgroup. Persons 10 and 14 each receive three nominations and so are more central in their subgroups than other members. In well-managed mergers and linkages, the central actors are connected to one another.

How these subgroups are connected, whether via marginal or central individuals, has important implications for diffusion of information. Figure 7-5 shows simulated diffusion when the information originates with randomly selected seeds and when the subgroups are connected four possible ways: disconnected,

FIGURE 7-4. Two Ways to Join Disconnected Divisions

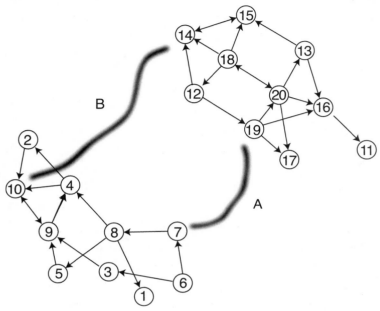

Source: Author.

connected through marginal members (link A above), connected through leaders (link B above), or connected randomly. When information originates in the network randomly and the groups are disconnected, information reaches less than half the overall network. For the three connected groups, however, the manner in which they are connected does not matter much in terms of diffusion. All three connected groups have about the same rate of diffusion with some divergence toward the end of the process. Thus, if one expects information to emerge in the organization randomly, how individuals are shared or move between agencies is of little consequence to overall performance.

FIGURE 7-5. Information Diffusion via Randomly Selected Seeds under Four Connection Scenarios

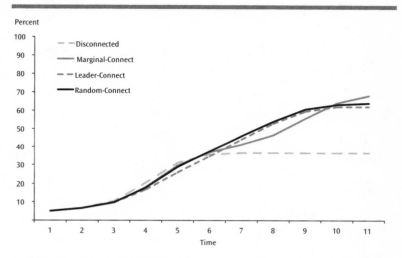

Source: Based on author's calculations.

Figure 7-6, however, illustrates what happens when information originates with leaders under the same four connectivity conditions. For the disconnected network, information originating with leaders again percolates to a fraction of the overall network, though this fraction is considerably higher (about 15 percentage points) than under the random origination condition. When the subgroups are connected by the leaders, information diffusion is considerably faster, as the darker dashed line shows, whereas the randomly connected and marginally connected subgroups experience much slower diffusion. When leaders perform the bridging function of connecting otherwise disconnected groups, they are very efficient at spreading information throughout the organization.

The simulations in figure 7-6 suggest that if directors want to achieve the fastest diffusion across separate subdivisions, they need

FIGURE 7-6. Information Diffusion via Leaders under Four Connection Scenarios

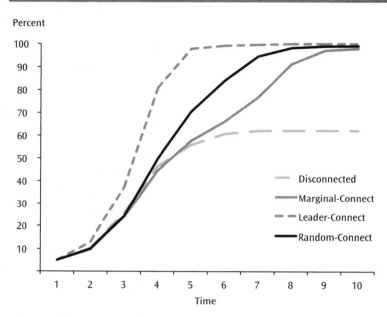

Source: Based on author's calculations.

to connect with network leaders within those divisions and have them be the originators of information. Indeed, department head meetings are created precisely for this purpose. Yet real world functioning within divisions in terms of disseminating novel information suggests that this practice is elusive at best.

Discussion

This chapter has attempted to outline and articulate some of the challenges that directors face when organizations have "silo" issues. Many organizations are composed of separate agencies or divisions that lack adequate interconnectivity. These gaps slow the spread of information that may be critical to overall organizational success. If critical information needs to be disseminated throughout the organization, using opinion leaders to spread that information yields large benefits in terms of how quickly the information spreads. In contrast, information that originates on the periphery of the network spreads much more slowly.

Leaders, however, cannot bridge disconnected groups, and so they are ineffective at transmitting information beyond their immediate domain or outside their host agencies. Indeed, novel information often originates on the network periphery because marginal actors have greater access to it and perhaps to other divisions within the organization. However, as the simulations demonstrate, relying on peripheral individuals to connect subgroups results in suboptimal conditions for spreading information and changing practices. In addition, if information originates randomly, then how subgroups are connected is of little consequence; diffusion occurs at the same rate regardless of how groups are connected (see figure 7-5). But when information originates with leaders, how subgroups are connected matters quite a bit. Subdivisions connected by leaders experience much more rapid diffusion when that information originates with leaders.

The challenge for within-group managers is to resist the temptation to send their peripheral employees to make contact with other divisions. The manager's temptation is to keep leaders within his or her own organization as they are vital to division performance and functioning. Yet this tendency has negative consequences for the overall performance of the broader agency because the linkages between groups are less valuable structurally and so do not provide good pathways for information to spread throughout the organization.

Notes

1. T. W. Valente, "Network Interventions," *Science* 337, no. 6090 (2012): 49–53.

2. T. W. Valente and R. L. Davis, "Accelerating the Diffusion of Innovations Using Opinion Leaders," *Annals of American Academy of the Political and Social Sciences*, no. 566 (1999): 55–67.

3. J. Lomas and others, "Opinion Leaders vs. Audit Feedback to Implement Practice Guidelines: Delivery after Previous Cesarean Section," *Journal of the American Medical Association* 265, no. 17 (1991): 2202–07.

4. T. W. Valente and P. Pumpuang, "Identifying Opinion Leaders to Promote Behavior Change," *Health Education and Behavior* 34, no. 6 (2007): 881–96.

5. R. Iyengar, C. Van den Bulte, and T. W. Valente, "Opinion Leadership and Social Contagion in New Product Diffusion," *Marketing Science* 30, no. 2 (2011):195–212.

6. P. Bonacich, "Power and Centrality: A Family of Measures," *American Journal of Sociology* 92, no.5 (1987): 1170–82.

7. G. E. P. Box and N. R. Draper, *Empirical Model-Building and Response Surfaces* (New York: Wiley, 1987).

8. E. M. Rogers, *Diffusion of Innovations*, 5th ed. (New York: Free Press, 2003).

8

Leveraging Networks through Boundary Spanning Leadership

DONNA CHROBOT-MASON, KRISTIN CULLEN,
AND DAVID ALTMAN

That's a great picture of our network showing all those connections, and we see some disconnects too, but I have to ask, what do we do now? *How* do we improve our networks and leverage connections to increase innovation?" These are questions we often hear from leaders who are viewing dramatic visuals depicting the network of relationships among their employees. Facing limited resources and complex challenges, they see a clear need for greater interagency collaboration and cooperation. Most accept that they simply have no choice but to work across boundaries to achieve their mission and goals. Thus it is clear that the majority of leaders recognize the value of network analysis to evaluate the collaboration and communication channels that crisscross their organization and reach out to other agencies. Network diagrams often illustrate clear gaps in communication and collaboration as well as indicate key individuals who serve as a bridge between groups. What is not clear, however, is what to do once gaps and isolated groups have

The authors would like to thank Tom Gaffney, Clemson Turregano, and Jennifer Martineau, at the Center for Creative Leadership, for sharing their experiences in helping organizations span boundaries.

been identified. How can such gaps be closed? What should be done to increase the strength of ties that support collaboration?

This chapter offers a model for addressing such questions. We present the boundary spanning leadership model and its accompanying strategies and practices as a way of addressing what leaders can do to maximize the potential of organizational networks and foster intergroup collaboration. Specifically, the chapter highlights three boundary spanning strategies and six leadership practices, and then illustrates this process model using examples from work with clients.

When Boundary Spanning Leads to Deeper Divisions

To begin, it is important to recognize that public sector leaders have long called for greater collaboration and integration across agencies, divisions, and levels. The need to enhance and coordinate the flow of information and resources across boundaries is not a novel idea or concept. But why then are most organizations not better at developing effective organizational networks and leveraging those networks for greater innovation and organizational transformation? Our research suggests that the answer may be our natural tendency to encourage the dissolution of boundaries. We often hear clients touting the need to operate as a single entity, to strive for unity in thought and purpose.

What this strategy fails to recognize is the need for individuals and groups to feel valued for their unique contributions and identity. Historically, many government agencies have operated in silos and competed with one another for scarce resources. Naturally, individuals have developed a strong identity and affiliation with their own agency. Such identification is a way for people to denote to themselves and others not just where they work, but who they are. Organizational psychologists have demonstrated that employees strive to meet two paradoxical needs in the workplace: being valued and recognized for their uniqueness while at the same time belonging to and feeling a part of the larger organization.[1] Leaders must balance these competing needs. Although it may be clear that continuing to work within silos is no longer effective and collaboration across boundaries is crucial to the success of the organization, dissolving long-established silos is often met with resistance, and collaboration across boundaries proves to be more difficult than imagined. We argue that this is because it is important to meet both the need for unity (belonging) and separation (distinctiveness).[2] A key point is that leaders must work to decrease identity threat and find ways to maintain subgroup identity while at the same time fostering greater collaboration. It is this process that we outline below.

Begin by Managing Boundaries

Although somewhat counterintuitive, our research as well as that of others suggests that boundaries must be managed before they can be spanned.[3] That is, before groups can share information and resources with other groups to contribute to a broader goal or mission, they must first develop their own group identity. They must ask themselves the following types of questions: What are our group's unique strengths, challenges, responsibilities, and resources? What type of work should we engage in to enhance the organization's mission, and what is better left for others to accomplish? What do we as a group value and prioritize given our unique vantage point in the organization?

The first step toward boundary spanning is to engage in a strategy we refer to as *managing boundaries*. It involves clarifying and defining existing boundaries. The focus is internal, and the goal is to create or strengthen a group's identity—its defining characteristics, values, strengths, and priorities. Differences are emphasized when managing boundaries to meet the need for distinctiveness or separation. Clarifying how one's group is separate from others allows for the recognition and valuing of differences. The initial step of encouraging groups to develop a strong identity and appreciation of differences lays the foundation for collaboration.

For example, consider two divisions of a large research and development (R & D) military organization that had entrenched cultures and a history of operating independently while ultimately supporting the same mission. It is no surprise that the merger of these divisions in service of efficiency and accelerating innovation was met with some resistance. Research on organizational mergers and acquisitions suggests that resistance and a reduction of productivity and effectiveness in the short term are very common occurrences. However, resistance may be mitigated and collaboration more likely to occur if identity threat is minimized and groups are valued for their previous identity. Failure to do so often results in polarization of groups as individuals struggle to maintain their sense of identity and unique value to the new organization or agency. The Center for Creative Leadership (CCL) had the opportunity to work with this organization during a time of significant transformation. Its leaders recognized the need to learn new ways of working together before work patterns and climate reset. They engaged in a workshop designed by CCL to lead participants through the six boundary spanning practices. As we describe these practices below, we will refer to our work with this organization to illustrate the boundary spanning process in action.

Boundary spanning begins with managing boundaries. From a leadership perspective, we emphasize two practices to foster strong network ties within a group. *Buffering* involves shielding a group from outside threats. For example, a leader may separate groups to minimize or remove external connections by locating all group members on a separate floor of the building or taking the group on a remote retreat. This physical separation creates the time and space for group members to focus their attention inward and develop strong internal relationships. The development of strong relationships among team members creates a dense network within the team. Dense networks foster trust, support, and cohesion. Buffering allows groups the time to answer the questions raised above, which helps members develop a clear group identity that includes a definitive and meaningful role within the organization. Reinforcing a group's role and associated decision rights also helps to clarify and in some cases necessarily fortify boundaries between groups. The process of buffering provides the foundation for intergroup collaboration by facilitating feelings of trust, support, and purpose within a group. If groups do not understand and feel secure in their own purpose and what they might bring to a potential collaboration, they may feel threatened when asked to collaborate and share resources. But once group members experience a state of psychological safety and security created via buffering and feel grounded in strong internal relationships, they can begin the process of reaching out to others.

Reflecting involves seeing both sides of a boundary and enabling others to see both sides as well. To see both sides of a boundary between groups, one must understand the needs, values, beliefs, and preferences of each group. In essence, one must understand each group's identity and present that identity to others without judgment or bias. This can be very challenging because it requires understanding the core of what each group is about and what each group needs. While the practice of buffering helps clarify group identity internally, the next step for leaders is to facilitate knowledge sharing across groups. This can be achieved in a variety of ways (such as communication sessions, exchange of values and mission statements, job shadowing, and rotation), but all require an openness and flexibility to understand and appreciate the differences that surface. Reflecting activities create the time and space for members of each group to share their group identity, understand one another, the boundary that divides them, and the complexities they face. Leaders should play an important role by asking questions that invite exploration of each group's identity and drive to the heart of why differences exist between groups and why these differences are central to each group's identity. The process of emphasizing differences may seem counterintuitive, but by gaining a deeper understanding of their importance, groups are able to build intergroup respect by accepting and valuing these differences. Furthermore, by digging deeper, group members discover similarities across the divide that had previously gone unnoticed. Understanding and valuing differences as well as identifying similarities set the stage to move forward together.

The Merger Experience

Work with the military R & D organization involved a two-day workshop. Though the newly merged divisions already had been colocated in their shared workspace for three months, it was important to begin by highlighting differences. Thus the morning session was spent in separate groups to provide time and space for individuals to reaffirm the identity of their "old" division and identify what they would bring to the new, combined division. Afterward, the two division groups were brought back together and invited to share with one another their aspirations for the new, combined division and what they would bring to the partnership.

Build Cross-Group Connections by Forging Common Ground

The second strategy we recommend to enhance boundary spanning is what we call *forging common ground*. Once group differences are clarified and valued, it is possible to then focus on similarities and begin to identify a common mission and vision. The goal is to build unity and meet organizational members' need for belonging. The need for belonging is often met when group members understand and share in the mission of the organization or agency. Fostering cross-group relationships and ties to accomplish the organization's mission and goals is the emphasis now. As a result, groups begin to seek opportunities for greater collaboration.

In practice, forging common ground involves fostering additional relational ties outside of one's group. From a leadership perspective, we emphasize two practices. *Connecting* involves developing person-to-person linkages through which trust is formed between individuals in different groups. Through the process of connecting, individuals deemphasize group identity–based differences and find similarities at an individual level. When people learn to know others as individuals and not simply as members of another group, boundaries between groups begin to fade. Positive sentiments develop as individuals identify commonalities at a personal level. The role of the boundary spanning leader is to create an environment where these personal connections can be made. For example, leaders can organize meetings or social gatherings in environments that are neutral for the different groups, develop areas in the workplace that are conducive to spontaneous conversations, provide communication technologies that allow individuals to learn about each other, and encourage individuals to spend time really getting to know coworkers outside of their group in order to develop the meaningful relationships that will form the linkages across agencies or divisions. As more and more individual relationships are formed, the density in the network between groups increases, and mutual confidence and trust between groups is built. Once intergroup trust is in place, groups can foster shared direction and begin to coordinate their efforts to achieve a common purpose.

Mobilizing involves crafting a common purpose and shared identity that is inclusive enough to resonate with members of different groups. Creating a larger identity, often achieved through a mutually valued vision, goal, or task, reframes the boundaries that once divided groups so that they surround everyone. This shared purpose motivates the coordination of resources required for collective action. While individuals begin to uncover common ground through the process of connecting, mobilizing moves beyond personal connections to the development of an intergroup community. When creating a shared identity (common purpose or goal), leaders must be careful to include all members, though members of different groups may connect with the vision or goal in different ways. Narratives and symbols are powerful ways for leaders to convey a new broader identity with which everyone can identify and a mission in which everyone can play a part.

The Merger Experience

In the workshop involving a military R & D organization, members from each division chose a metaphor for their vision of leadership, and through a series of conversations with individuals from the other division, they explained their metaphor and what they would personally do to make the future of the combined division a success. This connecting activity set the stage for mobilizing, which began to occur when the head of the new division and his direct reports reflected on what participants had heard and experienced thus far in the workshop. As a result of synthesizing the two divisions' unique sets of skills and aspirations, the leaders began to identify a shared set of goals and vision for the merger.

Leverage the Network by Discovering New Frontiers

Discovering new frontiers is the third boundary spanning strategy. It involves a mindset and organizational practices that simultaneously support and value both group differences and similarities. It is only through meeting people's needs for both unity (belonging) and separation (distinctiveness) that leaders can begin to fully leverage the potential for collaboration and innovation that exists within the organizational network.

In practice, discovering new frontiers involves utilizing relational ties to bring the capabilities of different groups to bear on a shared, interdependent challenge. From a leadership perspective, we emphasize two practices. *Weaving* involves interlacing distinct group boundaries (that is, integrating differences to achieve a common goal). Each group fulfills a unique role in a collaborative effort. The guiding mission is shared by the whole, but groups are encouraged to maintain their distinct identity and purpose. Leaders facilitate this process by fostering and encouraging multiple, layered identities: each group's unique capabilities and strengths are reinforced, valued, and integrated to achieve a shared goal or mission. A leader's role in weaving is to remove obstacles that would derail collective efforts and capitalize on differences by coordinating the roles and actions of the various groups to promote interdependence. For example, the leader may achieve this by setting goals that cannot be achieved by one group alone, valuing all perspectives, and facilitating conflict resolution when intergroup differences cause tension.

Transforming involves bringing groups together to discover emergent, new directions that result in the reinvention of intergroup boundaries and identities. The collective values, beliefs, and perspectives shared within a group may change in fundamental ways when different groups are brought in for the purpose of tackling a problem or creating a new vision. New frontiers are found through weaving and transforming, but while weaving maintains group distinctiveness when creating a whole, transforming sheds prior group identities in favor of future possibilities, which are often unknown. Leaders may facilitate the transformation of previous group identities and boundaries using many of the practices discussed previously, including bringing members from different groups together, focusing the larger group's attention on the future and new possibilities, and promoting discussions of core differences and similarities as a foundation for a new group identity.

The Merger Experience

During the military R & D workshop, participants were guided to begin the work of discovering new frontiers but challenged to view this not as a one-time event but rather a new mindset in which innovative opportunities for collaboration are explored in an ongoing fashion. During the final phase of the workshop, new groups were composed equally of members from both former divisions. Working across the boundary that had separated the two divisions, group members collaborated to identify the most critical challenges facing the new merged division and then to develop an action plan to tackle these challenges. The process of transformation began to take shape as members of the newly merged division became highly invested in their collective future. To represent greater collaboration moving forward, lanyards were bestowed by the head of the new division on each member in attendance. The blue lanyards took on significance as they symbolized a new common vision and merged division that incorporated the strengths and values of each group.

Boundary Spanning Leadership in Action

To further illustrate boundary spanning as a strategy and process to better leverage network connections, we present a recent example using a client of the CCL, the Robert Wood Johnson Foundation (RWJF). What follows is one case study from a community in Alabama that effectively used boundary spanning leadership as part of its action learning project. This case is illustrative of experiences across all eight communities receiving the intervention.

An overarching project goal in this Alabama community was to increase community engagement among the residents of one of the most vulnerable neighborhoods in the city. This neighborhood had great need for services and support, but year after year, they did not have an adequate voice at the community's "decisionmaking table." Using boundary spanning leadership techniques, the team of RWJF Fellows participating in CCL's sixteen-month leadership development program engaged in a process of getting a group of some of the most disadvantaged residents together to build a community garden at the county hospital. The hospital caregivers (doctors, nurses, administrators, janitors) worked side by side with patients—specifically the mental health patients—to design, plant, and tend the garden. An effort of this kind had never been attempted before. By being exposed to the boundary spanning leadership model, the RWJF Fellows came to understand that despite the fact that the community was underserved and underresourced, if they could effectively cross boundaries, positive outcomes could be achieved.

Once finished, the garden was completely sustainable by the members of the community and the hospital staff. Indeed, the participants were able to secure $22,000 in funding to expand the garden into a second phase with even more vegetables produced. The benefits were widespread and unanticipated. For example, there were home-bound mental health patients who had not left their house in years (except for doctor's appointments) who now rode the bus twice a day to work their "shift" tending the garden. The hospital's patients were finally eating fresh vegetables and feeling empowered and engaged in improving their own lives as well as the lives of others in their community. The sense of engagement in and empowerment over community outcomes had increased.

To provide a sense of how the boundary spanning leadership model played out in practice, what follows is an abbreviated summary of some of the activities. In planning the garden project, the various community group members used buffering and reflecting tactics by holding weekly lunch meetings. Hospital staff, patients, and members of various community-based agencies identified and then shared with one another their unique interest in creating the garden. The early weekly lunch meetings involved a great deal of listening to one another—sharing different perspectives and clarifying each group's unique role in the project's success.

Even though participants in the garden project maintained their own group identity (as hospital employees, patients, leaders of community organizations), over time, this diverse group was able to establish common ground and create an additional identity that represented their collective interests in the garden. By using connecting tactics, community members got to know each other and developed relationships that fed group cohesiveness and support. Each participant's personality, interests, skills, and resources were brought to the table. Mobilizing became evident as doctors, nurses, administrators, janitors, and community organizers worked alongside patients to determine the focus, objectives, and scope of the garden itself. Those who attended the meetings automatically became members of the "steering committee." As a result, a new shared identity across diverse boundaries began to form.

As the project continued, the group became more adept at integrating differences to achieve their shared mission. For example, one patient was especially good at getting other patients from a clinic to come to garden events. Another patient volunteer was a lifelong gardener with invaluable knowledge about how to sustain a productive garden. A hospital dietitian regularly provided comic relief and bottled water to group members. And, against all odds, the hospital's director of social work was the one person who could motivate a reluctant maintenance supervisor to provide assistance. Members began to weave their unique talents together in support of their broader goal. And as a result, and despite the diversity of the group, everyone benefited in some way through working on this collaborative project. Participants who did the actual "field-work" in the garden experienced increased levels of outdoor physical activity; those who seeded strengthened their fine motor skills and mental concentration. Those fortunate community members who ate the organic produce grown in the garden had fresh, healthy, nutrient-dense food on a regular basis. Transforming seems evident in the fact that those involved in this innovative project promoted the development of sister projects that may well lead to community gardens in other parts of the city in the future.

Leveraging Networks through Boundary Spanning Leadership

The examples provided in this chapter—a merger involving two divisions of a large military R & D organization and a community-based leadership development project funded by the Robert Wood Johnson Foundation—illustrate some of the potential that exists to leverage organizational networks through the boundary spanning process. By first managing boundaries, then forging common ground, the two merged divisions of the military organization achieved greater success by developing a common mission and vision. By identifying what each division could uniquely contribute to the merger, each group's strengths were leveraged. Likewise, participants in the RWJF project laid a solid foundation for long-term collaboration by using the boundary spanning model. Hospital staff and patients were able to strengthen ties both within and then beyond their identity group to develop connections between the hospital and the community where previously few had existed.

Additionally, over time, a new identity was formed as participants in the garden project formed new, strong relational ties that connected them to one another based on a shared vision.

In this chapter, we highlight boundary spanning leadership practices as a way to leverage organizational networks. Although research and theory on organizational networks has proliferated in recent years, more research is needed to clarify the role leaders play in altering, adapting, and improving organizational networks. The boundary spanning leadership model we have presented may help advance this line of thinking. The position boundary spanning leaders hold between two distinct groups is similar to some brokering positions commonly discussed within the organizational network literature. Brokers filter information between otherwise disconnected entities, often with an emphasis on personal gain. Boundary spanners may also engage in some filtering and buffering as described previously, but the objective of boundary spanners is ultimately to increase intergroup collaboration.

This chapter has described a process in which leaders play an important role in facilitating boundary spanning practices within their organization to leverage the power of network connections. Boundary spanning leaders effectively balance the need for separation and unity and are able to integrate group differences and similarities in service to a shared mission. They provide opportunities to develop and strengthen both internal and external group ties and relationships, that is, they manage boundaries before forging common ground and discovering new frontiers. Fostering organizational networks that support interdependence, collaboration, and innovation requires sustained efforts. The boundary spanning leadership model provides a guide to help leaders move from identifying a need for greater collaboration to creating the conditions in which meaningful and productive connections can develop.

Notes

1. M. B. Brewer, "The Social Self: On Being the Same and Different at the Same Time," *Personality and Social Psychology Bulletin* 17, no. 5 (1991): 475–82.

2. C. Ernst and D. Chrobot-Mason, *Boundary Spanning Leadership: Six Practices for Solving Problems, Driving Innovation, and Transforming Organizations* (New York: McGraw-Hill Professional, 2010).

3. Ibid. See also M. A. Hogg, D. Van Knippenberg, and D. E. Rast, "Intergroup Leadership in Organizations: Leading across Group and Organizational Boundaries," *Academy of Management Review* 37, no. 2 (2012): 232–55.

PART III

An Enterprise Approach to Leadership Development

9

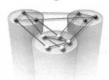

Building a Culture of Executive Collaboration

JIM TRINKA

M y current federal senior executive position in the Department of Veterans Affairs as executive director of the Leading EDGE program provides me with an interesting perspective on building and developing government-wide collaboration leading to improved enterprise leadership. The President's Management Council (PMC)—consisting mostly of cabinet-level deputy secretaries and some agency administrators, with the director of the Office of Management and Budget as chairman—approved the launch of an executive leadership training and development program called Leading EDGE: Executives Driving Government Excellence. Leading EDGE was inspired by the complexities and pressures of today's government, which increasingly require new levels of creative thinking and partnership. The program was conceived as an exclusive, executive-only network that unites the senior executive corps across the federal government in tackling America's greatest challenges (that is, "wicked problems"). In its design and focus, Leading EDGE would facilitate a free flow of ideas and agency spanning collaboration, and thereby take a major step toward creating a seamless and powerful senior executive corps, unified in purpose, aligned in priorities, and delivering better government performance to the taxpayer.

The 2012 inaugural year brought Leading EDGE participants together to interact with some of the best minds in the government, private, academic, and nonprofit sectors. They were challenged to approach problem solving in new ways; consider new government business and partnership models that focus on efficiency, effectiveness, and sustainability; and enhance their skills, test their assumptions, and look for innovative leadership opportunities. The collaborative nature of Leading EDGE provides an opportunity for senior executives to develop and expand their professional networks, a rich forum for discussion, an incubator space for innovation, and a continual learning environment that allows executives to test theories for improved performance. The investment in Leading EDGE demonstrates the critical value the PMC places on the role career federal executives play in leading high-performing government organizations and inspiring others to public service.

In leading this program, I learned a tremendous amount about enterprise leadership and why government-wide collaboration is so important. I met great leaders across government, many of whom succeed by practicing interagency collaboration. However, government-wide collaboration is difficult to achieve for several reasons: a culture that instills a transactional- versus relationship-based mindset, a system that rewards agency achievements versus interagency cooperation, a short-term focus on results based on limited-term political appointments, and precious little executive development opportunities to strengthen interagency collaboration. This environment makes government-wide collaboration and enterprise leadership difficult but not impossible. The rewards are great, but there are few consequences for noncompliance. Overcoming these limitations is precisely what is needed to strengthen enterprise leadership through collaboration in today's federal government and is the focus of this chapter.

Previous chapters have built a solid business case for the collaboration necessary to build and develop strong enterprise leadership. There are many leaders at all levels who demonstrate considerable expertise in enterprise leadership. The Partnership for Public Service annually awards Service to America Medals (Sammies) for noteworthy examples of enterprise leaders who achieve significantly positive results. I regularly attend the annual awards ceremony, and the Sammie award winners' stories are inspirational. I have met many of these leaders, and they all epitomize the characteristics of Level 5 leaders as described in Jim Collins's book *Good to Great*.[1] Humility and an unwavering focus on results are the competencies most often exhibited by these leaders. The significant accomplishments of these enterprise leaders create a sense of pride, admiration, and respect among the agency leaders who introduce the Sammie winners from their organizations. I have often witnessed a competitive spirit displayed by agency leaders who introduce and relate the stories of their own employees producing results across multiple government agencies. They tend to outdo one another in the description of their own folks, as if the accomplishments represented another competition. I think it is all good-natured fun, but it is also indicative of the system government leaders operate under.

How Sammie winners are able to succeed in this system is exactly what Collins's Level 5 leadership is all about. Leaders that are able to put aside agency competition and focus on results exemplify the characteristics of successful enterprise leadership. The Sammie award ceremony audience recognizes the winners' considerable accomplishments and leaves the event inspired to do more to create results in their own environment. However, they wonder whether they have the competencies necessary to succeed in this way.

Long ago, the senior executive corps was established to provide leaders across the federal government who could exercise Level 5 leadership on a daily basis. However, few executive development programs create the conditions for active learning in this environment. They do not provide practice on agency spanning challenges or instill an attitude of unified purpose or aligned priorities. No wonder the PMC felt that Leading EDGE was needed, not only to create a seamless and powerful senior executive corps but also to demonstrate the effectiveness of government-wide collaboration on tackling some of America's greatest challenges. Before describing some successful strategies for developing an executive culture of collaboration, I will explore some of the systemic barriers that inhibit enterprise leadership and make it difficult not only to develop but also to apply in the federal government.

First, American culture has been built on more of a transactional than a relationship mindset. Collaboration for Americans is more typically short term and related only to the transaction that is desired. That means, I will collaborate with you to produce a significant result, but it is for a specific purpose and not generally due to an established relationship. Ongoing relationships become somewhat secondary to successful transactions. Of course, there are exceptions to this behavior, but it is more dominant than people realize. Government departments that focus on international issues, such as State and Defense, know this phenomenon exists and train their employees specifically to counteract this tendency. From my time in the U.S. Air Force, I remember many training programs that focused on culturally sensitive behavior to facilitate successful overseas operations. They realized that a solid liaison was based on respect for cultural behavior because building the "relationship" was often more important than the transaction itself in a foreign environment.

Here is a poignant example that I heard of recently in the U.S. federal government that illustrates my point. An experienced executive was leading a project from an individual agency that necessitated considerable government-wide collaboration. A few federal government agencies, such as the Office of Personnel Management (OPM) and the OMB, typically focus on interagency issues requiring collaboration. A leader from one of these agencies suggested to the experienced executive that perhaps the project should be housed in the OPM or OMB rather than the individual agency where it currently resided, in order to take the project "to the next level." Presumably, the leader believed the only route to project success was through OPM or OMB leadership instead of the current arrangement in the individual agency. The experienced executive reacted in a predictable fashion and privately informed the leader that those remarks were not only a direct insult but also disrespectful. The leader never responded to the experienced executive's message, and quite obviously that leader truly believed there was only one pathway to success in this instance. This is the type of arrogance that typifies a transactional- versus relationship-based culture.

The second barrier that inhibits government-wide collaboration is the departmental configuration of the executive branch. Distinctive departments are established to focus on the various issues confronting the federal government in serving American citizens. Quite often these issues overlap and require considerable collaboration to best serve taxpayers. Many good reasons exist for this departmentalization, yet this situation has unintended consequences. Departments now compete for limited budgets, resources, and talent. One department's gain typically comes at a cost to another. As a result, leadership mindsets develop that favor individual agency interests rather than an interagency focus.

Some examples will serve to illustrate this point. Many government departments have the advancement of national and international commerce as important goals. Another government agency specifically has environmental protection as its mantra. A citizen would probably assume that considerable collaboration exists on these issues to further American interests. Quite often, however, that is not the case, and these government organizations sometimes operate at cross-purposes, competing with one another for funding, resources, and talent. Several Sammie winners avoided this situation and achieved success through collaboration. One played a key role in implementing the landmark Montreal Protocol, which has put us on a path to restoring the ozone layer by phasing out 95 percent of the world's ozone-depleting substances, and is leading current federal efforts to combat climate change. Another fostered a new breed of environmentally friendly construction and packaging materials that promote reuse, cut down on waste, and reduce greenhouse gas emissions. Enterprise leadership was difficult in these instances, yet it produced monumental gains.

The third aspect of our federal government system that somewhat inhibits collaboration is the short-term focus of political leaders brought into the executive branch as presidential appointees. Note that I am neither advocating for this to change nor asserting that senior executives cannot overcome this limitation, but I think it is worth mentioning as a potential barrier to government-wide collaboration. With the best of intentions, political appointees come in to lead government organizations and typically serve only two- to four-year terms. To make their mark on government, they take a somewhat short-term approach to achieve results they can tout as they depart their service tenures. Collaboration takes time as relationships build and therefore is sometimes sacrificed to achieve short-term agency results. Since career senior executives normally serve under political appointees, individual agency results can sometimes trump interagency achievements. It takes a special kind of political appointee or career senior executive to transcend this short-term focus, see the big picture, and achieve enterprise results. This is not by any means impossible, but it is difficult at best.

Again, an example may better illustrate this phenomenon. I have worked in many agencies when executive administrations changed hands, and many times one of the first strategies undertaken by new political leadership is organizational transformation attempted through departmental reorganization. Reorganizations, while often necessary and meant to elicit improved agency spanning coordination and results, take considerable research and time to plan and carry out. Often the reorganization is not fully implemented, and the expected benefits are not achieved within the time frame of the political appointee's tenure. New leaders inevitably replace the previous administration and change the focus of their leadership to other issues. Considerable time is thus consumed in the reorganization itself, and the anticipated improvements are rarely fully achieved. Considerable upheaval in the organization, caused by the transformation and reorganization, distract the agency's focus on positive results, and the American citizen pays the price of mediocre service. Yes, I am generalizing here, and good things can happen through reorganization, but often the full benefits are not realized. In general, the short-term focus of limited political leadership tenures can work against interagency collaboration and truly positive enterprise results.

The last systemic barrier to interagency collaboration is the genuine lack of executive development that focuses on the type of leadership necessary to carry it out. Few opportunities exist where executives can develop the competencies, skills, and attitudes that support strong enterprise leadership. The OPM's Federal Executive Institute (FEI) has the mission of executive development and does an admirable job of creating the environment where Collins's Level 5 executive leadership can be practiced, encouraged, and developed. However, the issue is not whether the FEI strengthens executive leadership and collaboration but rather whether it has the capacity to reach the quantity of leaders needed to make a difference.

The FEI's established brick-and-mortar presence in a location well removed from agencies' headquarters makes it difficult to fully develop the agency spanning collaboration required of a unified federal senior executive corps that delivers better government performance to the taxpayer.

The Leading EDGE senior executive leadership development program was created by the PMC in an attempt to deliver on that promise. In its inaugural year in 2012, Leading EDGE embarked on a unique cross-agency endeavor that provided federal senior executives with the skills and insights they need to thrive in a complex, rapidly changing environment. Leading EDGE successfully emphasized the importance of collaboration and innovative thinking to address government-wide challenges. The program brought together over 2,000 executives from sixteen agencies to enable them to enhance their skills, grow as enterprise leaders, and learn from one another. Participants took advantage of individual and team learning opportunities through six successful workshops, participated in two unique leadership assessments, and engaged in executive coaching. A new level of cross-agency collaboration was fostered through a series of Government Performance Projects that drew diverse teams from across participating agencies. All of this effort was coordinated and supported by a sophisticated web portal under the auspices of the OMB.[2]

The 2012 Leading EDGE program can claim tangible success. It brought leaders together from the public, private, and academic sectors to share their experience and provide participants with new insights into addressing tough organizational issues. After the final workshop, 90 percent of senior executive participants said they gained knowledge helpful in their jobs, and 87 percent said they would recommend the program to a colleague. Leading EDGE is conspicuously building a growing cadre of participants who have received the individual support and feedback they need to thrive as true enterprise leaders. The program depended on the critical feedback and involvement of participants, sponsors, and advocates to not only establish solid proof for the effectiveness of the Leading EDGE concept but also to promote the value of its unique status as a program for executives, by executives.

Leading EDGE provides a cogent example of the type of executive development necessary to strengthen government enterprise leadership. The program highlighted the accomplishments of true enterprise leaders who delivered positive results for the American citizen. Many Sammie award winners and other notable leaders who demonstrated interagency collaboration described their accomplishments to senior executive participants to demonstrate the power of an agency spanning outlook. Keynote speakers and expert panels related their experiences and challenged the participants to think outside their limited agency boundaries. Senior executives discussed these issues among themselves to learn from each other. These experiences were invaluable as methods of enterprise leadership development. Feedback obtained through network and leadership skills assessments on wicked government problems provided the standards for practicing interagency collaboration. Executive coaches focused on the true meaning of collaboration and the benefits of an enterprise orientation. Finally, action learning on executive teams that undertook difficult Government Performance Projects cemented the learning and provided the results that Leading EDGE promised. The pedagogy behind Leading EDGE's methodology for developing enterprise leaders capable of cross-agency collaboration shows merit and promises significant results, not only for individual agencies but also for the entire government in serving its citizens.

Sadly, development efforts in and of themselves offer only a small step toward strengthening enterprise leadership in the federal government. Without an unwavering senior leadership commitment to overcoming the existing systemic barriers that thwart interagency collaboration, the U.S. government cannot hope to positively change the status quo. The four barriers I described earlier present difficult challenges in and of themselves and, while not intractable, will take considerable effort to overcome. Building relationships needs to transcend the transaction-based culture inherent in America to further the benefits of true and ongoing collaboration. Rewarding interagency collaboration as much as, if not more than, individual agency results will set the standard for the desired enterprise leadership behavior necessary to address government's wicked problems. Lengthening the short-term focus of political leadership by concentrating on longer-term goals across government will expand the circumstances where cross-government collaboration flourishes. Finally, departmental commitment to invest in its leaders through development programs such as Leading EDGE will positively change the collaboration landscape.

I am reminded of some examples where agency leadership established new standards for executive leaders and undertook unique and, in my humble opinion, quite effective measures to ensure success. I was waiting in the lobby of the Nuclear Regulatory Commission for an escort to take me to a meeting with some of its executives. On the wall of the waiting room, a flat-screen television was showing a video of a town hall meeting of employees and leaders. Some tough employee questions were being fielded by the leaders, and promises were made to take action to resolve issues that negatively affected worker productivity. I cannot think of a better example of a low-technology and low-budget approach for visibly displaying leadership characteristics and competencies necessary to engage employees in the agency's work. My meeting with the executives was to plan executive development engagements to strengthen those competencies and skills. In the short span of an hour, I could clearly see why the Nuclear Regulatory Commission consistently scores in the top three of the "Best Places to Work" survey in government.

The formula for government agency action to achieve cross-government collaboration seems eminently clear: establish a new standard for collaboration, visibly demonstrate its success through leadership action, effectively communicate the new requirement to the entire organization, reward outstanding collaborative efforts, build on successes, and consciously develop leaders to not only positively change collaborative behavior but also sustain it. This recipe may sound like a typical change management exercise with a multistep approach to achieve the desired result. In fact, that is exactly what it is, and what better way to plan and implement the change than to follow some basic steps to "unfreeze" current behavior, implement the change, and then "refreeze" the desired behavior? Developing an executive culture of collaboration across organizational boundaries is the ultimate change management project. The effort is extremely difficult and requires significant intestinal fortitude, but the rewards are great. It would be nice if cross-government collaborative efforts were recognized more often than once a year in a Sammie Award ceremony. It could be an everyday occurrence given a strong will, a plan, and immaculate execution.

I once heard a keynote speaker say that maintaining a positive and enthusiastic attitude was essential for a leader to succeed in any endeavor. I initially thought it was a bit presumptuous and that attitude in and of itself would not make a tremendous difference. Hard work and effort are still important, right? As I listened to the speaker describe what he meant, I again thought of Collins's Level 5 leader. By the end of the speech, the speaker displayed through his words and demeanor and through the successful results of his organization that he was spot-on with his description. I left the event inspired to go out and make a difference and be enthusiastic and deliberate in my leadership actions and attitude. I am of the opinion that he is a very wise leader after all. I am also reminded of a sports company that has a familiar saying that sums up the lessons I am trying to convey here: "Just do it!"

Notes

1. Jim Collins, *Good to Great* (New York: HarperBusiness, 2001).
2. See MAX.GOV (https://max.omb.gov/maxportal/).

10

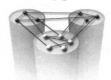

Developing Enterprise Leaders: The Case of the U.S. Intelligence Community

RONALD SANDERS

In this day and age, where crosscutting, "wicked" problems are the norm for many senior government executives, the case for developing more net-centric, enterprise-focused leaders—leaders who are able to overcome bureaucratic stovepipes to achieve *interagency* unity of effort—is compelling. However, in a federal government that looks more like a holding company than a seamlessly integrated enterprise, that turns out to be far easier said than done, often pitting the equities and interests of *individual* agencies against those that represent their *collective* missions.

The challenge is not just with overcoming organizational parochialism and politics, though as documented in the case study that follows, these can be powerful sources of resistance; it is also with the devilish details of an interagency leadership development system itself, administrative details like who is selected for development, who evaluates and rewards participants' performance, who gets to select the best of them for promotion, and so forth. These are details that are difficult enough to work out within a single department or agency, much less across several that do not share such things as a common chain of command or even common personnel rules.

The U.S. Intelligence Community (IC) offers a contemporary case in point. Beginning in 2005, the Office of the Director of National Intelligence (ODNI) led an unprecedented effort to design and implement a system specifically intended to develop and deploy enterprise-focused leaders across the IC, and in so doing, begin to break down some of the organizational stovepipes and insularity that led to the tragedy of 9-11. That multiyear effort, officially designated as the IC Civilian Joint Duty Program, was part of a broader, ODNI-led strategy to create a "culture of collaboration" in the IC, and it offers insights into the organizational and administrative lessons learned by the program's designers along the way.[1]

The Impetus for Change: A Burning Platform

The tragic events that transpired on 9-11 are all too familiar, and they need not be recounted here. In their aftermath, the nation, as is its custom, undertook a deep and difficult examination of what happened and why, with a particular focus on the apparent failure of the federal government's intelligence and law enforcement agencies to detect and prevent the attacks. That examination was conducted primarily by the National Commission on Terrorist Attacks upon the United States (also known as the 9-11 Commission), and one of its findings is most relevant here: it found that those intelligence and law enforcement agencies each had separate pieces of information that could have uncovered and possibly even prevented the terrorist plot, but they failed to share those pieces of information and were thus unable to "connect the dots" that would have revealed its contours.

Among the various reasons cited for that intelligence failure, the commission concluded that the IC lacked senior leaders who had the wherewithal to lead the *entire* U.S. Intelligence Community—that is, the U.S. intelligence "enterprise"—and in so doing, be able to know, understand, and most importantly, integrate *all* of the IC's intelligence collection and analytic capabilities to deal with the terrorist threat. The more-or-less contemporaneous Presidential Commission on Weapons of Mass Destruction in Iraq, the so-called WMD Commission, reached a similar conclusion, and both recommended a solution that had been tried and proven in the U.S. military: something called joint duty for the IC's civilian leaders-to-be.

The Legacy of Jointness

Joint duty and the larger concept of *jointness* had become embedded in the American armed forces, the result of the landmark 1986 Goldwater-Nichols Act, and the commissions specifically sought to replicate it in the IC. Those visionaries who drafted, debated, passed, and implemented Goldwater-Nichols knew that if the United States were going to win future wars, it would have to be led by senior military officers who were able to deploy and fight its land, sea, and air forces in an integrated, seamless way. To prepare those officers, the act required that as a prerequisite to flag rank, they would need to complete one or more joint assignments to the new, interservice combatant commands established by Goldwater-Nichols specifically to integrate and deploy the full panoply of U.S. military forces, as well as assignments to comparable "purple" organizations.[2] That requirement forced the development of enterprise-focused military leaders, and many attribute the phenomenal success of the U.S. armed forces during and since Desert Shield–Desert Storm to its unifying effects.[3]

That lesson was not lost on the drafters of the Intelligence Reform and Terrorism Prevention Act of 2004 (IRTPA), and they directed a similar approach in the IC. Specifically, the IRTPA mandated that the newly created position of director of national intelligence (DNI) "seek to duplicate joint [military] officer management policies established by . . . the Goldwater-Nichols Department of Defense Reorganization Act of 1986." To that end, the act authorized the DNI to "prescribe mechanisms to facilitate the rotation of [civilian] personnel of the intelligence community through various elements of the intelligence community in the course of their careers in order to facilitate the widest possible understanding by such personnel of the variety of intelligence requirements, methods, users, and capabilities."[4]

Further, it authorized the director to make such interagency assignments "a condition of promotion to such positions within the intelligence community as the Director shall specify," in an effort to mirror the military requirement established by Goldwater-Nichols.[5] However, as with Goldwater-Nichols, the real goal was culture change. In the U.S. military, it was to create a culture of *jointness*; in the IC, it was to foster a culture in which IC agencies and professionals would share information and intelligence—in other words, a true culture of collaboration.[6]

The program's hypothesis was that over time, the IC's agencies would be led exclusively by executives who had a broader, enterprise focus, and that their interorganizational networks, a by-product of their development as enterprise leaders, would facilitate the sharing of not only information and intelligence but also insights and ideas among agencies—precisely what *did not* happen in the months and weeks that preceded 9-11. However, this was far easier said than done, and despite the legislative and moral mandate, the challenges, administrative and otherwise, were considerable.

Enterprise versus Agency

Part of the challenge had to do with the IC's complex organizational environment. As of the passage of the Intelligence Reform Act, the U.S. intelligence enterprise comprised seventeen separate agencies, fifteen of which were organizationally "owned" by one of six cabinet departments (the remaining two agencies, the Office of the DNI and the Central Intelligence Agency were independent executive agencies that reported to the Executive Office of the President), and each of the secretaries of those cabinet departments enjoyed substantial statutory authority over their civilian and military personnel.

Moreover, the thousands of civilians employed by those departments and agencies were governed by five different statutory personnel systems, ranging from "regular" federal civil service rules covering civilians in the Departments of Homeland Security, Treasury, and State, to the almost limitless personnel flexibilities afforded the CIA and the ODNI. Each of those systems included its own senior executive service,[7] and by law and custom, those systems reserved the selection of senior executives to the heads of those departments and agencies.[8]

In contrast, the DNI's legal purview over those departments, especially with regard to personnel matters, was ambiguous, with the IRTPA authorizing the director to establish personnel policies (including those requiring interagency rotational assignments) but qualifying that authority by providing that it could not be exercised in a way that was inconsistent with the statutory prerogatives afforded cabinet secretaries.[9] Notwithstanding the relative ambiguity of his statutory authority, the nation's second DNI, J. Michael "Mike" McConnell (a former U.S. Navy vice admiral and director of the National Security Agency until he left for the private sector in 1998), made the establishment of a civilian joint duty program one of his top priorities when he was appointed in 2006. The IC's legislative mandate was clear enough in that regard, even though the DNI's legal authorities were not.

To be sure, most of the heads of the IC's various agencies and elements generally supported the concept of civilian joint duty—and the development of senior leaders with an enterprise focus—on its merits. This was especially true of the heads of DOD's largest intelligence agencies (like the National Security Agency [NSA], National Geospatial-Intelligence Agency [NGA], and the Defense Intelligence Agency [DIA]), which were all headed by general or flag officers who themselves had had to complete one or more military joint assignments as a prerequisite to flag rank, pursuant to Goldwater-Nichols.[10] However, support for applying that same concept to civilian senior executives did not necessarily (or easily) translate into the creation of a system for developing enterprise leaders in the IC, and it took the intelligence community almost two years of intense interagency coordination and collaboration to resolve the myriad issues underlying its design, development, and implementation.

What Would Qualify as Civilian Joint Duty?

Perhaps the most fundamental detail in that process involved the definition of joint duty itself. What kinds of assignments would count? Which would most contribute to the development of enterprise leaders?

This was a seminal question, and it required policymakers and program designers to strike a balance between the ideal and bureaucratic reality. The U.S. military's approach was instructive but ultimately proved unworkable for the IC. The DOD actually maintains a list of joint military assignments that number in the thousands, involving tours in the department's several regional combatant commands, the Office of the Secretary of Defense, or the Joint Chiefs of Staff. In addition, the development of enterprise leaders in the military was enabled by centrally managed (and directed) officer assignments, regular rotation cycles, an "up or out" promotion system at the general officer level, and most significantly, a decades-long tradition of investing in the preparation of officers for generalship.

That kind of enterprise leadership pipeline was problematic for the IC's civilian executive ranks. For example, the IC's various agency-centric civilian executive development systems had none of the institutional advantages of the military system, nor was there a sufficient number of rotational assignments in the IC's relatively few "joint" organizations, like the National Counterterrorism Center (NCTC) or the ODNI itself, to fill the pipeline. Accordingly, the IC's agencies agreed to a much simpler, default approach, that is, that almost *any* interagency assignment—from one IC agency or element or equivalent to another, at a position of comparable pay grade or rank—would suffice.[11] After all, at its most basic level, the joint duty program was intended to foster the development of executive candidates who had an enterprise perspective and the boundary spanning networks that came with it.

The IC also agreed that such interagency assignments would be at least one to three years in duration, on the premise that anything shorter would not give individuals on joint duty sufficient understanding of the agencies to which they were assigned (including their missions, structure, key personnel, and cultures) as well the opportunity to build lasting collaborative relationships while on that assignment.[12] In addition, the IC also determined that certain assignments *internal to a particular IC agency* could also provide the experiential equivalent of a joint duty assignment outside of that agency, to the extent they involved significant responsibility for interagency, interdepartmental, or even international programs or operations—for example, as an agency liaison to one of the DOD's combatant commands, the dozens of FBI-led Joint Terrorism Task Forces in major U.S. cities, or international organizations like NATO.

Taken together, these various measures were intended to give as many IC professionals as possible the opportunity to serve in an enterprise capacity, and in so doing, begin to build (person by person and assignment by assignment) the interagency collaborative networks and enterprise-wide perspective that would ground an IC culture of collaboration. However, with these broad parameters, the number of potential candidates who would be eligible for and interested in those assignments numbered in the tens of thousands.

How Would Candidates Be Selected for Joint Duty?

Given that an interagency assignment was eventually going to be required for promotion to virtually all senior executive positions, and because the number of interagency opportunities that offered such joint duty experience was relatively small compared to the pool of interested and eligible IC employees, the program's designers assumed that each joint duty opportunity would be coveted— and likely draw dozens of highly qualified candidates. As a result, the IC readily agreed that selection for those precious few "feeder" assignments would be subject to merit-based competition. However, that laudable policy had unintended consequences.

To operationalize that policy, the IC agreed that when an agency was willing to offer up one of its vacant positions as a joint duty opportunity, it would advertise that vacancy on an intranet site specifically set up by the ODNI for this purpose. Once posted, *two* separate rounds of competition would ensue. First, each agency would conduct an internal competition to select one or more "highly qualified" individuals from among those of its employees that applied for the vacancy. Those finalists would then be referred for consideration to the IC agency advertising the opportunity (this was designed to spare the latter from being inundated with applicants). Thereafter, a second, final round of competition was conducted by the advertising agency to select the "winner" from among the candidates referred to it by all of the agencies.

Needless to say, while merit principles were well served by those two rounds of competition, the time it took for them to run their course became problematic, and that "fill lag" was further compounded by the time it took for the selectee to actually report for the joint duty assignment. Add to that the time it took for the receiving agency to reimburse the donor agency for the costs of the employee selected for the temporary assignment (a statutory requirement for long-term temporary assignments between agencies), and the timeline from start to finish—that is, from a joint duty vacancy announcement to an employee actually reporting for that assignment—became untenable.

Thus merit-based competition became a significant disincentive, limiting the number of joint duty opportunities agencies were willing to advertise. However, ODNI's NCTC piloted an alternative that seemed to effectively address these various administrative delays. Given that the NCTC's several hundred funded positions were to be staffed primarily by personnel on one- to three-year reimbursable rotational assignments from the various IC agencies, the aforementioned administrative delays had the potential for significant operational impact. Accordingly, instead of filling those positions on the same ad hoc basis as the rest of the IC, the NCTC negotiated annual aggregate staffing quotas with each of the agencies designated to contribute staff.

Those quotas also established in advance the amount of reimbursable funds the donating agency could expect—ensuring those contributing staff a steady, predictable flow of funds *from* NCTC that they could then use to prepare additional personnel to replace those on temporary rotational assignment *to* the center. When those personnel on joint duty returned to their home agencies, others were queued up and ready to replace them at the NCTC. It required the NCTC and agencies that contributed staff to manage those personnel rotations to and from the center, but with preestablished staffing quotas, standard joint duty tour lengths, and predictable funding, this proved far less complicated and far more expeditious than an ad hoc approach. Indeed, it was so successful that in late 2010 the IC Executive Committee considered expanding it to drive most joint duty staffing, but the process has not been extended beyond the NCTC to date.

How Would Employees on Joint Duty Be Evaluated and Promoted?

Another of the contentious issues confronted by the designers had to do with the annual performance appraisal of employees while on joint duty. Who would rate their performance and if otherwise warranted, be responsible for rewarding them with a bonus or permanent promotion? Before the advent of joint duty, the employees temporarily assigned from one IC agency to another had always been evaluated, rewarded, and promoted by their "home" agency.[13] This was because the IC's various agencies each had (and jealously guarded) its own unique performance management system, with different rating levels and definitions, performance standards, rating cycles, and perhaps most importantly, cultural norms—which is another way of saying that some agencies were historically more conservative while others were more generous when it came to performance rating rigor.

Performance bonus policies were just as disparate, with some agencies offering substantial, up to five-figure bonuses for a relatively small number of top performers while others applied a more egalitarian approach in their bonus policies, giving many more employees smaller awards. And at one extreme, one of the IC's largest agencies had never seen fit to offer bonuses to employees based on their annual performance ratings, emphasizing "on the spot" rewards for one-time acts of distinction instead. Thus there was little uniformity across the IC with respect to performance management policies and practices, and this lack of uniformity had implications for the joint duty program.

On one hand, there was the concern that an agency's highest performers would likely be wary of taking a rotational assignment in another agency if it meant adapting to a completely new performance management regime for one or more rating cycles; that argued for maintaining the status quo. On the other hand, employees who had completed an interagency assignment under the joint duty program's predecessor complained that their performance ratings (completed by their home agency) suffered while on those assignments—for example, many felt they were "out of sight, out of mind"—and that, in turn, negatively affected their chances for permanent promotion upon return to their home agency.[14]

The obvious solution was to implement a uniform IC-wide performance management system, but in the ODNI's early days, this drew too much agency resistance. Accordingly, after much discussion and debate, the IC agreed that an employee on joint duty should be evaluated along with his or her "new" peers—based on the same performance standards and by the same supervisor responsible for the performance of their entire work unit.[15] This would alleviate the "out of sight, out of mind" concern. However, to ensure that the employee's home agency would be able to understand and fully credit a performance appraisal received while he or she was on joint duty (since it was recorded on another agency's appraisal form, using different rating levels and standards), the employee's joint duty supervisor would be responsible for "translating" the evaluation onto the appraisal form of the employee's home agency.

This represented a substantial administrative burden for the employee's joint duty supervisor: the receiving supervisor would literally have to complete two evaluations for that employee, one using his or her agency's own form and policies and one using the unfamiliar form and standards of the employee's home agency. After this onerous policy had been in effect for just a single annual appraisal cycle, the IC's agencies concluded that the administrative burden was simply too great and determined that greater interagency uniformity was appropriate, a proposition that had been unthinkable at the start of the design process.

As a result, after a surprisingly brief interagency coordination cycle, the ODNI issued an IC policy directive (ICD 651, *Performance Management System for the IC Workforce*) establishing a common set of performance management policies and procedures—including uniform rating levels and definitions, performance standards, process requirements, and rating cycles—for all IC agencies and employees, largely to ensure the consistent treatment of employees on joint duty. Agencies could still customize their respective performance management systems to reflect their missions and cultures, as long as they remained consistent with those "core" requirements, but in effect the IC had established a uniform interagency performance management system—the first of its kind in the federal government.

In contrast, the IC left the responsibility for making permanent promotion decisions in the hands of the individual agencies, including promotions to those senior executive positions that required joint duty. Agencies would retain their own unique promotion systems—ranging from traditional vacancy-by-vacancy approaches in the Departments of Homeland Security, State, and Treasury, to military-like promotion boards in the CIA and the NSA—but they did agree to a uniform set of promotion standards for all senior executive positions.[16] As an added protection, IC agencies agreed to report senior-and-below promotion rates to the ODNI to ensure that employees who were on or had completed an interagency assignment were being promoted at an *overall* rate comparable to their peers. However, this still left the ultimate payoff of the joint duty program—promotion to senior rank—in the hands of the individual agencies.

Who Would Be Authorized to Waive the Joint Duty Requirement?

The single most contentious issue faced by the IC involved the right to waive the joint duty requirement in any given senior promotion action. The implications were obvious and significant. Agency officials, especially those representing DOD, asserted that since their agency heads had the unequivocal statutory authority to select individuals for senior positions in their respective agencies, they also had the inherent right to waive the joint duty requirement in those selections or to exempt certain positions from the requirement altogether.[17] And not surprisingly, the DNI found that position untenable, given the history of joint duty waivers in the U.S. military and notwithstanding his ambiguous statutory authority. There the matter stood for months, leaving the joint duty program in limbo.

It was not until a change in leadership occurred at the very top of the IC that this dynamic began to change. Defense Secretary Donald Rumsfeld resigned in early 2007, along with his under secretary for intelligence. Rumsfeld was replaced by former CIA director Robert Gates, who in turn brought in former Air Force lieutenant general James Clapper as his under secretary.[18] Ambassador John Negroponte, the first DNI, also resigned and was replaced by McConnell, who as head of the NSA in the 1990s had worked closely with Gates and Clapper. And Negroponte's principal deputy, Air Force General Mike Hayden, also a former NSA director and a contemporary of Jim Clapper, was named to head the CIA.

Thus, when Director McConnell declared from the outset of his tenure that the joint duty program would be one of his highest priorities, his past and present colleagues were willing to help him succeed—even if that success were to come at the expense of some of their respective organizations' heretofore "sacred" equities, like waiver authority. Indeed, since DOD's legal authorities had posed the most significant roadblock to resolving this issue, DNI Mc-Connell made a personal plea to Secretary Gates for flexibility in that regard, and because of their long-standing relationship, Gates responded favorably. They, in turn, instructed their representatives to find a way to resolve the impasse over joint duty waivers, and they did.

Starting with the premise that the DNI should retain independent authority (de facto, if not de jure) to waive the joint duty requirement, the designers drafted language that would vest joint duty waiver authority in a newly created position subordinate to the DNI: the director of defense intelligence. And as part of the agreement, the under secretary of defense for intelligence (James Clapper) would be "dual hatted" in that new position. Thus, if the director of defense intelligence ever exercised that authority, he would be doing so as an authorized representative of *both* the DNI and the secretary of defense.[19] This administrative legerdemain allowed both the DNI and the secretary of defense to say (primarily to their own lawyers!) that their respective and potentially conflicting statutory authorities remained intact—in effect, each had the authority to waive the joint duty requirement, albeit vested in the same dual-hatted individual.

Implementation to Date and Lessons Learned

After almost two years of interagency collaboration and coordination, implementation of the IC Civilian Joint Duty Program has been fully under way since 2007, with the joint duty requirement phased in to cover all senior positions on and after October 2010, and by most accounts, significant progress has been made toward its primary objective: an IC senior leadership corps that is truly enterprise-oriented in composition and outlook.[20] Well over 75 percent of the IC's hundreds of senior executives now have some form of credible interagency experience, and perhaps more importantly, well over 15,000 IC professionals below the executive level also have joint duty credit, thus ensuring a pipeline of leaders-to-be who also share an enterprise perspective and the boundary spanning, interagency relationships that go along with it.

It is not yet clear whether this is sufficient to sustain a true culture of collaboration across the IC, but at least the IC's professional and leadership corps is no longer characterized by stovepiped, agency-centric experts and executives. Thus the IC's approach to developing enterprise leaders, born out of the tragedy of 9-11 and forged over many months of (sometimes contentious) interagency coordination and collaboration, can serve as a potential model for other interagency "enterprises" across government.[21] However, there are some important lessons to be learned from the program, not only with regard to some of the administrative details that the program's designers ultimately devised but also from the process that led to their resolution.

Lesson 1: Administrative Details Matter

First and foremost, it is clear that the success of any program to develop enterprise leaders, especially one that includes relatively long-term interagency rotational assignments as one of its principal features, depends on a comprehensive administrative infrastructure—that is, all of the detailed rules that will govern how candidates for the program are selected for interagency assignment, how their participation is funded, how they are evaluated and rewarded during their assignment, and ultimately whether and how they are promoted into senior leadership positions. It is especially critical early, when the enterprise program is nascent, and individuals who volunteer for it do so at some potential (or at least perceived) risk to their careers. In effect, those details serve as an insurance policy for these "early adopters."

These often mundane details are difficult enough to resolve within a particular agency, but they become even more challenging in an interagency context, where those taken-for-granted agency prerogatives may have to be compromised to serve the interests of the larger enterprise. In that context, administrative details become aggrandized, symbols of an agency's institutional "rights" and the closer the enterprise's interests come to infringing on those fundamental prerogatives, the harder compromise becomes.

In the case of the IC, those administrative details were eventually codified in an IC directive (ICD 601, *Joint Intelligence Community Duty Assignments)* issued May 16, 2006, one of the very first issued by the fledgling ODNI, and it took almost a year to develop. However, it lacked such critical details as an actual implementation timetable or an oversight and enforcement mechanism, nor did the directive come to grips with the issue of joint duty waivers—that took another thirteen months to resolve, with the release of detailed implementing instructions in June 2007. Together, these issuances established the requirement that joint duty experience would be a *mandatory* prerequisite for promotion to almost all senior IC positions, and in so doing, they established a foundation for developing enterprise leaders in the IC.

Lesson 2: Incentives (and "Teeth") Are Critical

The relative success of the IC joint duty program, measured by the number of midlevel professionals, managers, and senior executives who have had an enterprise (that is, interagency) developmental experience, can also be attributed to the ultimate incentive established by those policy issuances: that is, that interagency experience was a condition precedent to promotion to senior rank. This was the secret to the success of Goldwater-Nichols and the U.S. military's version of jointness, and it was also at least one of the reasons for the failure of the IC joint duty program's various predecessors—the fact that while they encouraged interagency assignments, there was no certain reward for the risks and burdens involved, both individual and organizational.

Thus promotion to senior rank was the program's ultimate incentive, and DNI McConnell and the program's designers knew that if agency heads could waive the joint duty requirement, the program would be on shaky ground. Especially given the less than successful history of the civilian joint duty program's predecessors, they were concerned that many employees—especially those high-performing leaders-to-be who were already on track to become senior executives in their respective agencies—would not incur the career risk associated with a lengthy interagency assignment, protections and oversight notwithstanding.[22] Instead, they could (and probably would) "play the odds" and avoid the burdens and uncertainties of joint duty, hoping that when their chance came to compete for a senior promotion, their agency head would simply waive the requirement.

With independent waiver authority vested exclusively in the Office of the DNI, the opportunity to game the system was virtually eliminated, and to date, the ODNI has not even been asked to grant a waiver, thus ensuring the program's "value proposition" to those who aspired to be senior executives in the IC. By that measure, the waiver compromise was clearly worth the contentious discussion and debate that preceded it. However, to complement that administrative arrangement, the ODNI also established a number of program performance metrics—including the number and percentage of senior executives with joint duty credit, the number of employees on interagency assignments at any given time, and their relative promotion rates—to aid program oversight and evaluation. These too provide "teeth" to the program insofar as they offer visibility into each agency's promotion patterns and early warning if those patterns suggest that an agency's leadership pipeline is not sufficiently joint.

Lesson 3: Senior Leader Engagement Is Critical

This gives rise to the third lesson learned from the IC effort: that is, the importance of senior leadership engagement, especially from those senior leaders who come to the table with an enterprise perspective themselves. As noted, this was the case in the IC, where DOD's intelligence agencies were all headed by general or flag officers who themselves had had to complete a joint assignment as a prerequisite for flag rank. In addition, Air Force General Mike Hayden brought that same perspective with him when he became CIA director, as did FBI Director Robert Mueller.[23]

Their conceptual support was leveraged via such nascent collaborative "platforms" as the IC Executive Committee—composed of the heads of its agencies and elements—and supporting Deputies Committee, as well as by the IC Chief Human Capital Officers Council. These entities helped when it came to those "red line" issues that affected agency equities and authorities that had to be addressed at the most senior ranks of the IC, and in the case of joint duty waivers, even at the cabinet level. As recounted above, that was the ultimate red line issue, and it took the personal intervention of Defense Secretary Gates and DNI McConnell to resolve the matter. Only their network of relationships (between Gates and McConnell, McConnell and Clapper, Gates and Clapper) made this work.

Without those trusted relationships, the arrangement regarding joint duty waivers would not have been acceptable, legally or otherwise. And in terms of the ability of the IC to sustain the joint duty program's progress to date, the good news is that many of the senior leaders involved in establishing it (such as FBI Director Mueller) remain in office and in some cases are in positions of even greater authority. For example, former DOD under secretary of intelligence and director of defense intelligence James Clapper is now DNI, former DIA deputy director Leticia Long is now director of NGA, and former CIA associate deputy director Michael Morell is now the agency's deputy director. Thus, despite the joint duty program's somewhat ambiguous statutory underpinnings, not to mention its long and sometimes contentious development, the personal involvement of these enterprise leaders ensured each of their agency's commitment to the final result—and to the program's long-term sustainability.

Conclusion

The benefit of having the most senior agency officials—not just human resource officials, but those with *overall* agency leadership responsibility—so deeply engaged in the program's design cannot be overstated. However, even that is not enough to guarantee its long-term prospects. Despite the progress that has been made to date, a program as far-reaching and potentially controversial as the Intelligence Community Civilian Joint Duty Program remains fragile, even after almost six years in full effect. Like its military progenitor, the program requires individual agencies to subsume their parochial interests—especially with regard to their discretion to develop and promote their own senior executives—and as such, it has not yet reached taken-for-granted, institutional status.

That was the conclusion reached by the Government Accountability Office (GAO) in 2010, in its first-ever foray into IC management matters. It found that despite unprecedented strides, the IC's joint duty program—perhaps the federal government's first-ever concerted effort to truly develop a cadre of enterprise leaders—had lost some of its early momentum.[24] Among other things, it found that

—the program lacked a strategic framework to guide its further implementation,

—the ODNI had not used the various program performance measures described above to evaluate the efficacy of the program and revise it as necessary,

—turnover and downgrades in the leadership of ODNI's joint duty program office had hampered the program's maturation, and

—the ODNI had not finalized a promised leadership and executive education curriculum to ensure that individuals who were on or had completed an interagency rotational assignment had the opportunity to reflect on that experience.

While the ODNI took exception to these findings, they cannot be discounted completely. Coupled with the lessons learned from the program's early days, as discussed above, they offer a cautionary tale for those who would take on the development of enterprise leaders elsewhere in the federal government.

Notes

1. The author served in the ODNI as associate director of national intelligence and IC chief human capital officer for the IC during this period of 2005 to 2010 and was one of the principal architects of the system.

2. "Purple" is a Pentagon euphemism synonymous with "jointness" and allegedly comes from what one gets when the colors of the various military service uniforms are blended together.

3. It is notable that before and immediately after passage of Goldwater-Nichols, the joint duty requirement was strongly resisted by the military services.

4. For the legal language of the IRTPA, see "50 USC § 403–1 - Responsibilities and Authorities of the Director of National Intelligence" (www.law.cornell.edu/us-code/text/50/403-1).

5. Ibid.

6. The second DNI, Vice Admiral J. Michael McConnell, coined this term to describe the goal of the joint duty program as well as that of a number of other initiatives designed to incentivize information sharing across the IC.

7. The Senior National Intelligence Service (covering ODNI executives), the CIA's Senior Intelligence Service, the "regular" Senior Executive Service (SES), the FBI's separate SES, the DOD's Intelligence Senior Executive Service, and the Senior Foreign Service.

8. While the qualifications of those appointed to the SES by a cabinet secretary have to be reviewed and approved by the Office of Personnel Management (OPM), that approval has been largely pro forma; thus the OPM rarely denies a senior executive selection. Note that most of the IC's executive appointments are not covered by OPM rules and are thus exempt from that review in any event; SES-equivalents in the ODNI, CIA, FBI, and DOD's IC agencies (National Security Agency, National Geospatial-Intelligence Agency, Defense Intelligence Agency) are appointed directly by their agency heads.

9. Section 1018 of the IRTPA.

10. As had DNI McConnell in his military career.

11. For example, an assignment to the National Security Staff at the White House, a NATO partner, or Interpol would count; additionally, certain intergovernmental, private sector, nongovernmental, academic, or other professional experience could also qualify for credit.

12. As a deployment incentive, joint duty credit was awarded for a six-month assignment in a designated combat zone; in addition, an individual could meet the one-year minimum through a series of consecutive or nonconsecutive ninety-day interagency assignments, as long as those shorter assignments were completed within a two-year period.

13. This included employees who had participated in the IC joint duty program's predecessor, the IC Assignments Program (ICAP); see note 14.

14. Twice before, in the early and mid-1990s, the IC had officially encouraged interagency assignments for similar purposes and had even created an IC Assignments Program (ICAP) in 2003 to facilitate them. However, those efforts had little impact on the IC's senior leadership corps since they did not require IC agencies to give an individual's interagency assignment any weight in the promotion process, and as of 2005 (when the ODNI was established), only a few hundred IC professionals, mostly from the DOD, had completed the ICAP's requirements.

15. The recipient agency would also determine whether an employee on joint duty would receive a performance bonus, with funding for such bonuses being the responsibility of that agency.

16. Intelligence Community Standard (ICS) 610-1, *Core Qualification Standard for Senior Civilian Officers in the Intelligence Community*, issued on February 22, 2010 (signed by the author in his previous ODNI capacity).

17. For purposes of this discussion, I treat the a priori exemption of certain positions (typically, those that are one of a kind or that require esoteric, hard-to-find technical qualifications) from the joint duty requirement as synonymous with waivers—that is, cases where the senior position requires joint duty as a prerequisite but where an authorized official waives that requirement so that an individual without prior joint duty could be promoted to that senior position.

18. Note that Under Secretary of Defense for Intelligence Clapper had previously headed two DOD intelligence agencies, the DIA and NGA.

19. To avoid any legal challenges to the waiver provisions, the designers incorporated so-called treaty language in the draft implementing instructions whereby each agency head and department secretary stated that they *voluntarily* agreed to exercise their statutory authorities in a manner consistent those instructions—and in so doing, technically preserved their statutory authorities, including the discretion to void that agreement at any time.

20. For example, in 2009 the program received the coveted Innovations in American Government Award from Harvard University's Kennedy School of Government.

21. The still nascent National Security Professional Development program, established by Executive Order 13434 in 2009, can be traced to the IC program, and it served as the basis for Senator Joseph Lieberman's proposed Interagency Personnel Rotation Act of 2011 (S. 1268), introduced in June 2011.

22. See note 14.

23. Director Mueller had already instituted a rigorous internal mobility policy for senior agents that included foreign deployments and assignments to the DNI's NCTC. He viewed interagency assignments to other components of the IC as simply an extension of that policy and entirely consistent with his own post-September 11 strategy for developing senior FBI leaders with a broader interagency focus.

24. In a compromise reached with Congress during deliberations leading to the fiscal year 2013 Intelligence Authorization Act, DNI Clapper agreed to permit the GAO to review certain management issues in the IC, and its June 2012 evaluation of the IC's joint duty program was one of its first efforts in that regard. See GAO, "Strategic Approach and Training Requirements Needed to Guide Joint Duty Program," GAO-12-679, June 20, 2012 (www.gao.gov/products/GAO-12-679).

11

Interagency Rotation Programs: Professional Development for Future Enterprise Leaders

LAURA MILLER CRAIG AND JESSICA NIERENBERG

W icked problems—entrenched, complex, multifaceted issues—require collaborative solutions. Collaborative solutions require leaders who can think and act across organizational lines. How then do we equip our government leaders with the tools to work across agency boundaries to achieve what is best for our nation?

Interagency Job Rotations Can Develop Enterprise Leaders

While conducting research at the Government Accountability Office (GAO) on interagency collaboration in the national security arena, we found that job rotations were often cited as a powerful tool to develop enterprise leaders: agency executives who understand strategic goals, problems, and prospective solutions from a big-picture, whole of government perspective.[1] One of our reviews focused on

The authors wish to thank Elizabeth Curda, J. Christopher Mihm, Melanie Papasian, Erin Saunders Rath, Albert Sim, Bernice Steinhardt, and Kate Walker, who made significant contributions to the Government Accountability Office (GAO) work that serves as the basis for this article. While drawn from GAO work, the material in this article has been sufficiently modified so that the views expressed are those of the authors and not necessarily those of the GAO.

three interagency rotation programs operating in the federal national security arena: two managed by the Department of State and one by the U.S. Army's Command and General Staff College (CGSC) at the Department of Defense (DOD).[2] As part of this review, we surveyed the programs' participants and host supervisors to get their perspectives on outcomes and other aspects of these programs. Overall, the survey responses indicated that these programs serve as an effective means of developing enterprise leadership skills. For example, 83 percent (sixty-four of seventy-seven) of participants who responded reported that the programs were "very effective" in helping them to develop their abilities to consider national security issues from a broad-based, interagency perspective. In addition, 86 percent (sixty-six of seventy-seven) reported that these programs were "very effective" in helping them to develop skills to lead in an interagency environment.[3]

Sending current or future leaders on assignments at another agency can help them develop across several dimensions.

Foundational Knowledge

On an interagency assignment, an individual can establish a common foundation of shared knowledge for understanding partner agencies' roles, responsibilities, authorities or capabilities, or specific subject matters. Working with personnel at other agencies can further reinforce a common vocabulary or framework for understanding complex policy issues. This is important for facilitating collaboration among personnel who may normally approach issues from different perspectives. For example, in the national security arena, personnel from diplomatic, defense, commercial, or law enforcement backgrounds may have disparate views on a given issue.

Collaboration Skills

Depending on the assignment, an individual can build specific skills needed for interagency collaboration, such as how to plan, lead, and execute interagency efforts. Several experts contend that the best way to teach people to lead in a collaborative environment is to provide them with an opportunity to do so.

Interagency Networking

Interagency assignments can promote networks among personnel from the host and home agencies. Job rotation programs can be designed with a formal component to encourage networking, or networks can be established informally through day-to-day inter-actions between the individual and his or her peers at the host agency.

Interagency Job Rotation Programs Are Difficult to Design and Manage Well

On the face of it, sending future leaders from one agency to an-other seems like a common-sense way to break down organiza-tional boundaries—a means of razing those infamous agency "silos" that stand in the way of collaboration and enterprise lead-ership. The assumption is that once an official from one agency walks a mile in the shoes of another agency official, mutual under-standing improves and the groundwork is laid for future coopera-tion. Why, then, are interagency rotation programs so few and far between in the civil service?

The answer to this question may lie in the challenges to design-ing and managing such programs well. Our research indicates that there are three main actors who must invest in the program and whose needs must be satisfied: the individual participant, the home (sending) agency, and the host (gaining) agency. A successful pro-gram must provide an adequate return on each actor's investment (see figure 11-1).

FIGURE 11-1. Successful Interagency Rotation Programs—A Win-Win for Participating Individuals and Organizations

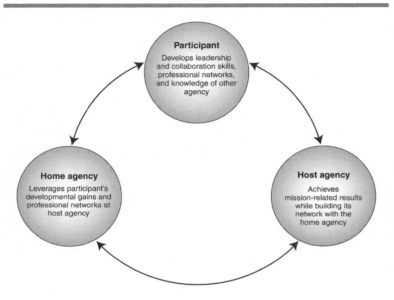

Source: GAO, *Interagency Collaboration: State and Army Personnel Rotation Programs Can Build on Positive Results with Additional Preparation and Evaluation*, GAO-12-386 (March 2012 www.gao.gov/assets/590/589170.pdf).

Interestingly, many rotation program failures described in the literature and by human resources practitioners seem to reflect cases where the program was designed primarily to benefit only one of the actors—sometimes inadvertently at the expense of another. Here are some examples.

—Home agency managers expressed concerns based on past experiences that even though rotations may benefit their emerging leaders, giving up these "superstars" temporarily to another agency leaves managers with critical workforce gaps. In the case of programs that are designed as personnel exchanges, some managers described instances where they sent their strongest individual and received a poor performer in return. In either case, home agency managers are still responsible for accomplishing their missions without the high-performers that went on rotation.

—Host agency managers expressed concerns about the time it takes to bring rotation participants up to speed on their assignments. Rotating personnel cannot always make a contribution to the host agency immediately and may need time to learn about the organization, the people, and the specific assignment at hand, depending on the complexity. In addition, host agency managers noted that their agency may have to invest a significant amount of time to provide mentorship or formal training. Finally, some managers said they had no control over who would be assigned to them or whether the individual would have appropriate experience and skills to perform effectively in the rotation.

—Individuals expressed concerns that rotations may not actually provide them with professional opportunities, either to develop their skills or subject matter expertise, or to advance their careers. Several described instances where their skills were not used or they did not learn much because they were simply being used to plug a workforce hole at the host agency. Moreover, many individuals were concerned that they would miss out on promotion opportunities at their home agencies because their home agency's chain of command may not be aware of or value their contributions at another agency.

Our research also pointed to other, broader challenges. Because rotation programs involve multiple parties and organizations, there can be extensive logistical complications associated with timing of the rotation and reentry, selection processes, performance appraisal systems and procedures, and numerous other factors. It is also necessary to avoid the appearance or reality of one agency "owning" the program because this can compromise the program's credibility and effectiveness in ensuring benefits for the other participating organizations. This can be especially complicated in the federal government, where funding streams and authorities tend to be directed toward a single agency. In the national security arena, where rotations often involve DOD's military services, it can be difficult to avoid the appearance that DOD controls the interagency programs since the military services dwarf civilian agencies in terms of size, resources, and dedicated time for training and education. Finally, managing and participating in such programs is typically time and resource intensive.

Another complicating factor in designing and managing a successful rotation program is that the program may impose costs and confer benefits on different parts of a participating organization. For example, while the host agency manager who sends his emerging leader for a rotation may incur the cost of a temporary workforce gap, the host agency's leadership may reap the benefit of having a stronger pool of prospective leaders with an enterprise, whole of government perspective.

Design Strategies and Management
Practices for Successful Rotation Programs

The GAO has reported on several design strategies and management practices that can lead to a successful rotation program for emerging enterprise leaders. Many of these strategies and practices are intended to address the challenges described above and to ensure that all of the participating actors—at the individual and organizational levels—receive a return on their investment. They are as follows:

—Design the program to achieve overarching or shared strategic goals by involving prospective participants and the host and home agencies in the program development. The goals of the program—and how achievement of these goals will benefit each actor—must be clearly articulated. Because a rotation program combines learning and practice, it can be designed to achieve a range of mission and workforce development goals. For example, a program could be designed to help the host and home agencies achieve common mission goals, such as improving reconstruction outcomes in a particular nation. At the same time, the program can also be designed to provide participants with interagency experience leading to a whole of government perspective, and in the longer term, shore up the host agency's pool of prospective enterprise leaders.

—Provide individuals with incentives to participate by factoring rotations into promotion decisions, harnessing internal motivations, recognizing and rewarding accomplishments and good performance outside their home agencies, and providing public recognition for program participation.

—Provide management—at host and home agencies—with incentives to participate by minimizing coordination issues that can make a rotation difficult or time-consuming to manage, rewarding managers who support interagency rotations, and providing host agency managers with high-performing staff. This is particularly important to address the challenge that line managers often bear the cost—but do not directly reap the benefit—of supporting a rotation. Rotation programs that develop enterprise leadership abilities may primarily benefit the individual, the agency, and the government as a whole. Therefore, program designers may need to engage the highest level of leadership—at the agency level or above—to determine how to incentivize managers to support rotations.

—Optimize the match between the participant and the assignment by ensuring host agency needs and participants' professional needs are taken into account when defining assignments and assigning positions.

—Prepare participants and their host supervisors for the rotation by providing orientation training or materials. Orientation materials could include information on the goals of the program, roles and responsibilities of the participant and supervisor, and key aspects of the host agency's structure, mission, and responsibilities, as well as the administrative aspects of rotating, such as how to be reimbursed for travel.

—Plan for the participant's next assignment to maximize benefits to the participant and the home agency. Encouraging periodic contact between participants and home agencies can help agencies identify the participant's skills, knowledge, and networks and plan in advance how to make the best use of them. Regular contact can also help to allay participants' concerns that their home agency management will forget them while they are on rotation.

—Create a program feedback and evaluation process that includes participants and all participating organizations.

A Case Illustration: U.S. Army Command and General Staff College Interagency Fellowship Program

One of the three interagency rotation programs we reviewed— CGSC's Interagency Fellowship Program—illustrates how many of the design strategies and practices described above were employed to overcome specific challenges and to bring about success. The Interagency Fellowship Program was one of the few such programs operating in the federal national security arena during our 2011 review. This program places army officers in intermediate-level positions at other federal agencies for ten to twelve months. First piloted in 2008, the program was designed to achieve multiple objectives that would benefit the individual participant, the host agency, the CGSC, and the U.S. Army as a whole. The program was to provide fellows with valuable professional developmental experiences and

Figure 11-2. Interagency Students Join Military Students in a Class at the Army Command and General Staff College

Source: GAO, *National Security: An Overview of Professional Development Activities Intended to Improve Interagency Collaboration,* GAO-11-108 (November 15, 2011). Photo: Noah Albro, Army Command and General Staff College.

grow their enterprise perspective and leadership abilities while increasing the workforce capacity of the host civilian agencies. In turn, partnering civilian agencies, such as the Department of State or the U.S. Agency for International Development, were often able to send civilian personnel to teach or attend courses at the CGSC (see figure 11-2).

CGSC program officials work with host agencies to address any potential governance issues that could be cumbersome for host agencies or that could discourage their participation. For example, CGSC officials use memorandums of agreement to detail roles and responsibilities, salaries and additional costs, selection criteria for participants, performance accountability provisions, and security clearance requirements, among other considerations.

In addition, CGSC officials adopted several practices to ensure they are sending high performers to host agencies. For example, the CGCS widely publicizes the announcement for the program and instructs its review board to identify the highest performers among the applicant pool. In 2011, 140 officers applied to the program to compete for twenty-eight available positions, allowing program officials to select their "best and brightest."

To further incentivize high performers to participate, the program was designed to ensure that participants (fellows) would be recognized and rewarded within the army, even while the fellow was away on rotation. For example, the host agency supervisor was required to complete a formal performance appraisal that was incorporated into the participant's army personnel record. Also, fellows are required to write a paper suitable for publication based on their experiences at the host agencies. This writing assignment encourages fellows to synthesize what they learned on rotation and how their newly acquired knowledge might be applied in future assignments. It also provides them with a career-enhancing opportunity to publish.

To help create a good match between the participant and the assignment, the CGSC used the application process to identify participants' developmental goals and professional interests. The CGSC also used its memorandums of agreement to identify specific skills and capabilities the host agency was seeking.

The program provided orientation training for participants to prepare them for their rotation. Topics included information on the program's background and objectives, how the rotation fit in with the CGSC's academic requirements, and the CGSC's expectations of each participant. CGSC officials work with partner agencies to create orientation materials for host supervisors that can help them prepare to manage rotations to achieve the greatest possible benefits.

The CGSC maintains contact with participants while they are on rotation. Career managers reach out to fellows before the end of their assignment to discuss their transition to a new assignment or their return to their home agency. CGSC officials reported that the fellowship program is seen as a long-term investment in officer careers, and even if immediate post-rotation assignments do not fully leverage a participant's interagency experience, future assignments are likely to include interagency positions.

CGSC program officials seek quarterly program feedback from participants each year, which they use to modify program processes and educational certifications. At the time the GAO published its review of this program, the CGSC did not evaluate the outcomes either for host agencies or for the army, nor did it collect feedback from host agency supervisors. However, CGSC officials reported that they intended to conduct follow-up surveys to capture longer-term results of program participation.

Conclusion

Our work has shown that interagency rotation programs can instill the collaboration skills and enterprise perspectives that future leaders need to address the wicked problems of the twenty-first century. However, these programs are not easy to design and manage effectively, and can impose significant costs on the individuals and organizations involved. Cultural differences that exist among different agencies, funding streams, and authorities that flow toward a single agency rather than toward enterprise-level goals are additional factors that complicate agencies' abilities to work together to design a win-win program. Establishing clear-cut goals for the program—and ensuring that these goals are in the interest of all parties—is critical for success because, in many cases, the goals serve as the incentives for both individuals and organizations to participate.

Several provisions of the 2013 National Defense Authorization Act are intended to expand interagency rotations and address some of the issues that can challenge their success. The act establishes an interagency rotation program for certain national security personnel and requires that the program be designed by an interagency committee chaired by the Office of Management and Budget. This framework may help ensure that program goals and incentives reflect the needs of the participating individuals and agencies and are aligned with the interests of the U.S. government as a whole.

Developing an interagency rotation program for national security personnel will be challenging and initially resource intensive. If designed and managed effectively, however, such a program could help shape a cadre of future leaders with the knowledge, skills, and networks to bring about better outcomes for the nation.

Notes

1. For more information, see GAO, *National Security: An Overview of Professional Development Activities Intended to Improve Interagency Collaboration*, GAO-11-108 (November 15, 2011).

2. See GAO, *Interagency Collaboration: State and Army Personnel Rotation Programs Can Build on Positive Results with Additional Preparation and Evaluation*, GAO-12-386 (March 9, 2012).

3. For the full survey instrument and results, see GAO, *Interagency Collaboration: Survey Results of State and Army Personnel Rotation Program Participants and Their Host-Agency Supervisors*, GAO-12-387SP, an E-supplement to GAO-12-386 (www.gao.gov/special.pubs/gao-12-387sp/).

12

Reinventing the Senior Executive Service as an Enterprise Asset

STEPHEN T. SHIH

Throughout the early part of the twenty-first century, the United States has continually faced major challenges that have been historic in their complexity, scale, and ownership by multiple nations and organizations. The sophistication and global nature of these challenges have resulted from numerous current societal and environmental factors: technological advances have made the world smaller by efficiently connecting vast numbers of organizations and individuals across great distances, commonly establishing and enabling larger, more complicated, and more collaborative ventures; evolutions in business, trade, economic development, and foreign relations have increasingly generated issues and impacts cutting across multiple nations, creating far more interdependencies and partnerships; medical and nutritional crises and natural and man-made disasters have frequently generated international rather than regional or local consequences; and military conflicts and terrorist threats have typically involved multinational situations and concerns. In order to best address these modern challenges, the U.S. government and each of its federal agencies must operate as part of a consolidated enterprise (composed of the federal government, state and local governments, the private sector, and other nongovernmental organizations), unifying and coordinating responsibilities, assets, and efforts to optimize scale of effort and mission effectiveness—particularly in an era of severely constrained resources. This enterprise-wide approach requires enterprise leadership—including from an enterprise-oriented senior executive corps, with the ability to lead collaborative efforts across the enterprise and capable of being deployed across the enterprise to provide leadership where needed.

The History and the Past of the Senior Executive Service

On October 13, 1978, the Civil Service Reform Act (CSRA) of 1978 (P.L. 95-454) became effective, creating the U.S. government's Senior Executive Service (SES)—a cadre of executive leaders across federal agencies responsible for strategically leading the operations and continual transformation of the federal government. The CSRA established the SES with the goal of creating a corporate cadre of leaders with shared values, a broad perspective of government, strong executive skills, and mobility across federal agencies.[1] The CSRA stated that the purpose of the SES was to "ensure that the executive management of the government of the United States is responsive to the needs, policies, and goals of the nation and otherwise is of the highest quality."[2] The federal government's senior executives would occupy the government's seniormost career positions, provide direct support to political leaders appointed by the president, and lead staff in each federal agency to carry out the president's priorities. SES members would be held accountable for individual and organizational performance, and to support this purpose, the CSRA gave greater authority to agencies to manage their executive resources while assigning the U.S. Office of Personnel Management (OPM) responsibility for government-wide leadership, direction, and oversight of the SES.

The Present State of the SES

In many ways the current SES has changed from the original enterprise vision that precipitated its creation in 1978. Each federal agency has been delegated human capital management authority over the SES positions allocated to each agency. Consequently, each agency recruits and selects individuals for its SES positions (selectees not previously appointed to the SES would still have to be evaluated and approved by a Qualifications Review Board administered by the OPM). In addition, each agency

—has broad discretion on SES training and development,

—is authorized to set pay for each of its SES members (within a general range) and to implement its own performance management system and awards, and

—has a unique mission, organizational structure, management philosophies, and resource levels.

Therefore each agency manages its senior executive resources in a different way than the others.

As a result of this decentralization in human capital management and the highly technical nature of many agencies' missions, combined with the complex challenges of the modern era, agencies sometimes recruit SES members with a focus more on technical proficiency than leadership and more on executives' qualifications to succeed within the specific employing agency rather than across the entire government. Agencies also have trained, managed, and recognized their SES members by narrowly concentrating on the senior executives' effectiveness and contributions to their employing agencies. This agency-specific focus and the investment employing agencies make in recruiting and developing their executives can serve as disincentives for employing agencies to support the movement of their SES members. Thus senior executives in the federal government have become more of an agency-specific rather than a government-wide resource, with bounded skills and knowledge and without the mobility and transferability of leadership across the government the CSRA originally intended.

The Future of the SES: Restoring the Vision of the CSRA

The federal government can best position the nation to prepare for and solve the wicked problems of the twenty-first century by realizing a key, original intent of the CSRA and reestablishing the SES as a government-wide cadre of executive enterprise leaders. This enterprise cadre must consist of the best and brightest leaders of our nation—individuals with exceptional strategic leadership skills, capable of developing and maintaining enterprise-level strategic vision, managing day-to-day operational demands in different organizations and positions across the government, while effectively acting and directing others in complex situations across the government and in other enterprise sectors that often become involved in complex, multinational crises and homeland security emergencies. These SES leaders must have a strong understanding of the need for enterprise connectivity and jointness of responsibility and action required to optimize the federal government's operations and performance. Such senior executives also must possess the competencies and proficiencies that would allow them to effectively influence collaborative action and build coalitions across the public, private, state-local, and nongovernmental sectors.

Given these needs, what kind of framework would enable the SES to return to its originally intended mission?

Option 1: Centralized Management of the SES

One way to achieve an enterprise-oriented SES cadre is to centralize the management of the SES; however, this approach is not easily implemented and also potentially includes some significant drawbacks compared to the current state of SES management. Centralization would involve consolidating executive resources control and human capital management into a single coordinating organization (for example, the OPM) able to standardize philosophy, policy, and practices on the recruitment, selection, development, performance management, compensation, and recognition of all SES members in the federal government. This standardization could then drive the consistent recruitment and selection of candidates who have demonstrated enterprise-level mastery and results, involving the highest level of executive core qualifications, and thereby ensure that selectees, upon appointment, will be immediately capable of providing enterprise executive leadership throughout the federal government. Standardized management would focus SES development and training on enterprise leadership learning and competencies supporting executive enterprise leadership and mobility. Standardized performance management, pay decisions, and awards also would promote an enterprise corps of SES members who are managed, compensated, and recognized in a consistent manner—accountable and incentivized for contributions and results involving the success of the enterprise.

However, centralized management of the SES may not be attainable or helpful for a number of reasons. For example, this type of wholesale reinvention of the SES may involve an extremely disruptive and lengthy transition that would be detrimental to the federal government's effective operations for a substantial amount of time. As noted earlier, agencies also have invested a great deal of time, effort, and resources into the selection and development of their SES members and likely will be strongly resistant to relinquishing any control of those executive resources or the actual positions or executives themselves. As also previously mentioned, the technical nature and focus of agency missions—and arguably of certain highly technical positions within agencies—also provide persuasive reasons and needs for agencies to maintain the control and presence of their executive-level leaders, who have technical expertise and familiarity with agency-specific culture and operations. Moreover, a single organization assuming responsibility for enterprise management of the SES will require a significant new allocation of funding and staff to support this new responsibility; this additional budgetary and resource allocation would presumably come from either new appropriations or reallocations of each agency's current funding and staff to the coordinating agency, neither of which may be politically feasible. A less disruptive and costly alternative could involve a hybrid approach with complementary centralized and decentralized models. Such an approach could involve the creation and staffing of an enterprise senior executive cadre that would be centrally managed and deployed to locations and programs to support the administration's highest priorities while preserving the current agency-specific management of SES members serving in positions allocated to each agency. However, this would still require the resolution of certain funding and control issues, including the budgetary and staffing needs of the coordinating organization, as well as issues arising from the loss of agency control or from the conflict or overlap in programs or initiatives for which specific agencies traditionally and legally have responsibility.

Option 2: Enterprise Leadership in a Decentralized SES Management System

The most feasible solution to achieve an enterprise SES cadre may be—appropriately enough—through enterprise leadership itself. Rather than centralizing the management of an SES cadre—that is, a top-down control structure that may not be attainable precisely because of the very "siloed" nature of federal agencies and their resources that drives the need for enterprise leadership—the requisite standardization and consistency of the SES corps may be better achieved through in-agency development of enterprise leadership to promote coordination and consolidation of individuals, resources, and action across silos. In this way, exceptional enterprise leaders can drive collaboration and unity of effort by each agency to apply consistent approaches to the leadership, operations, and maintenance of an enterprise SES cadre, including in critical management areas such as strategic planning, financial management, and human capital management. Agencies would potentially be able to reach consensus on key administration priorities, programs, goals, and metrics for the allocation and responsibilities of SES members. They would consolidate and collaborate on consistent approaches to fund SES positions and initiatives, and also apply common approaches to human capital management of senior executives.

The OPM is currently striving to provide enterprise leadership in the human capital management of the SES. In recent years, the OPM has especially concentrated on developing human capital policies, products, and services to unite and drive consistency in the federal government's management of its executive resources, while respecting and supporting agencies' delegated authority and discretion to manage the senior executive positions specifically allocated to them.

In recruitment and staffing, the OPM's regulations detail requirements for outreach, notification, and merit staffing, and it has collaborated with agencies to produce new methods of recruitment (for example, a streamlined, resume-only applications process) to reach a broader applicant pool, including private sector executives with enterprise leadership experience and skills. The OPM also has implemented innovations to the administration of its Qualifications Review Board—a standing cohort of SES members across the federal government who serve appointments of three months or more—to approve for new appointment to the SES only those candidates selected by agencies that have demonstrated the government-wide executive core qualifications evidencing the candidates' capacity to lead and be mobile across the enterprise.

Next, the OPM has produced enterprise resources and guides on executive development including an executive onboarding framework and guide; an executive development best practices guide; a supervisory training framework and guide; a training evaluation field guide; an online training and development "wiki" page (consolidating the most pertinent federal training and learning authorities, resources, and solutions); and HR University—an online portal providing human capital management training courses and products, including on leadership development.

The OPM also has supported and collaborated with the White House on a number of interagency executive development programs—with the participation of private sector chief executive officers—to support enterprise leadership training as well as an enterprise approach to training the federal government's SES cadre. Moreover, the OPM has issued regulations to standardize agency design and implementation of SES Candidate Development Programs, and agencies are required to obtain OPM certification before operating the programs.

Finally, the OPM provided critical enterprise leadership to coordinate collaboration on the design of a new standard SES performance appraisal system, issued on January 4, 2012. The design process itself united the cooperative efforts of federal agencies, the private sector, and nongovernmental organizations—consolidating activities, assets, knowledge, and philosophies while focusing diverse and multiple elements across the enterprise on a crosscutting enterprise solution. As a result, the new appraisal system constitutes an enterprise success and provides a new tool embraced by all federal agencies to drive a consistent, enterprise approach toward the performance management of all SES members across the federal government. In turn, this new system will enable different federal agencies to symbiotically promote enterprise senior executive leadership and the accomplishment of enterprise priorities and results.

Summary

The United States faces ever-growing challenges, requiring enterprise preparation and responses. This wide cooperation is particularly critical in light of current exigencies and priorities requiring federal agencies and organizations with different missions, cultures, and operational mandates, and under severe resource limitations to quickly achieve coordination, efficiencies, and forceful action through unity of effort. The U.S. government's senior executives—those serving in the highest-level career leadership positions across the government—must be capable of providing enterprise leadership throughout the government to promote collaboration and joint action throughout the nation. Consequently, these SES members must be recruited, selected, developed, and managed in an enterprise manner, and thus will the original vision of the SES be fully realized, better enabling the United States to meet the "wicked" challenges of the twenty-first century.

Notes

1. See Federal Jobs Network, "Senior Executive Service History" (http://federaljobs.net/ses_history.htm).
2. Ibid.

13

Meeting the Enterprise Leadership Challenge

JACKSON NICKERSON AND RONALD SANDERS

I f there is one thing that is abundantly clear from the research that led to this book, it is that wicked government problems— that is, those complex, crosscutting national challenges that require the integrated efforts of multiple government departments and agencies—are here to stay. No longer the exception to the rule, they are becoming the "new normal" for many federal managers and executives, most of whom are ill-prepared for them.

Our government indeed is fortunate to have enterprise leaders like Mike McConnell, Thad Allen, and Pat Tamburrino, as well as Steve Shih, Ron Sanders, and Jim Trinka, all contributors to this book. These leaders successfully tackled wicked problems that spanned multiple agencies with distributed authorities. Whether it was the post–September 11 integration of the intelligence community, the aftermath of Hurricane Katrina and the Deepwater Horizon oil spill, or the challenge of helping our veterans find jobs in a difficult labor market, these capable leaders stepped up to the task, utilizing the common goals, shared experiences, and networks of trusted relationships they had developed over their careers to make unprecedented progress against formidable bureaucratic odds.

The irony is that only some of these successful enterprise leaders were actually developed with those interagency challenges in mind. For example, Mike McConnell learned about leading "jointly" early in his military career, as did Thad Allen, both benefiting from the legacy of Grenada and the Goldwater-Nichols Act. However, for the most part, their colleagues had no such formal preparation and instead had to learn (sometimes painfully) through on-the-job training. The fact of the matter is that but for the uniformed military, and more recently the intelligence community, the federal government's leadership corps is decidedly agency-centric, stovepiped in terms of both orientation and skills. For the most part, they are developed, and in essence captured, by their particular federal department, bureau, or agency to lead that organization, without understanding, consideration, or incentives for contributing to the larger federal enterprise.

This agency-centric focus is traditional, the way government leaders have always been developed. As an aside, one could argue that the approach has not been particularly successful, at least if you believe the results of the Office of Personnel Management's latest Federal Employee Viewpoint Survey: the overwhelming majority of the tens of thousands of employees responding expressed alarmingly low trust and respect for their senior executives—and as budget woes force cuts in already meager agency leadership development budgets, those numbers are just going to get worse.[1] The purpose of this book, however, is not to critique agency-centric approaches to leadership development. Rather, it is to highlight what we believe to be an even more compelling set of emerging, *enterprise* leadership challenges and to propose an approach that will deliberately develop, promote, and retain leaders who are up to tackling those challenges.

With the proliferation of wicked problems, flat or declining budgets, the long-awaited tsunami (or at least a really big wave) of retirements among experienced senior managers and executives, and a political environment that denigrates if not demonizes civil service, we believe there is a debilitating deficit—a crisis—of enterprise leadership talent, perpetuated by a system of human capital development in the federal government that is fundamentally flawed in its ability to systematically grow enterprise leaders. Without a cadre of enterprise leaders on the job and in the pipeline, the federal government will be unable to successfully respond to the wicked challenges facing the United States in the twenty-first century. And as the government struggles, and increasingly fails, to successfully tackle wicked problems, the public's confidence in its government will be further eroded, creating a vicious "death spiral" of reduced support for funding, reduced capabilities, and even lower confidence.

A More Systematic, Enterprise Approach to Leader Development

Our goal in this concluding chapter is not to spell out a variety of doomsday scenarios stemming from the enterprise leadership gap. Instead, we want to examine what we have learned from the contributors to this volume, as well as from conversations with government leaders (many of whom have been students of ours in the leadership seminars we teach), academics, consultants, and educators, and synthesize a set of proposals that addresses the flaws of the existing approach to leadership development so that the supply of enterprise leaders is considerably and consistently increased. Toward that end, the proposals we offer below are based on three critical assumptions:

—Given the challenges facing our nation, the federal government needs to increase the supply of enterprise-qualified leaders.

—It takes years and careers to build enterprise leadership skills, as well as the cross-agency networks of trusted relationships and an enterprise-wide identity that enables them to develop; it is not something that happens during a few meetings or over a few months.

The development of enterprise leaders will not happen "naturally"; rather, it requires Congress and the federal government (especially the Office of Personnel Management [OPM]) to adopt a new leadership development paradigm, along with the policies and practices to make it a reality.

We believe that few will argue with our first assumption. All one need do is read tomorrow's headlines (in print or online) to conclude that the really wicked problems that face our nation, and hence our government, just do not fit neatly into the bureaucratically specialized, vertical structure that typifies the executive branch today. Rather, those wicked problems cut a horizontal swath across government's vertical boundaries, and they require concerted, collaborative action on the part of a whole host of federal (not to mention state, local, international, and nongovernmental) agencies that may share a common mission but little else. And yet those agencies are led by senior managers and executives who were developed, selected, and rewarded for their narrow, vertical expertise. That approach simply won't cut it.

The second assumption is based on our personal and professional experience, as well as the literature and practice of leadership development: we know it takes years, both on the job and in the classroom, to build the competencies, networks of trusted relationships, and reputation needed to be a successful enterprise leader, especially for an enterprise as large and complex as the U.S. government. Indeed, if the reflections of the enterprise leaders who contributed chapters to this book offer a guide, then developing the skills, networks, reputation, and trust needed for interagency leadership success takes many years and experiences and accumulates over a career.

Equally important is the idea that the government and the nation as a whole benefit from a career executive corps with an enterprise mindset rather than executives that pursue parochial goals within their particular agencies. However, it is also clear that an enterprise-wide identity must be established early in a developing leader's career and should be continually reinforced (by selection, evaluation, and promotion) throughout it.

Our third assumption has two parts. The first, that enterprise leaders have to be developed deliberately, is obvious. The second, that Congress and the executive branch must act to establish a system that will do so, may not be as evident to leaders of those institutions. It is this view that we hope our book can help advance. We believe that small tweaks to the existing, agency-centric approach to leader development in the federal government will *not* produce the enterprise leaders needed now and in the future.

The current system, if one can call it that, has been around for almost half a century, unchanged since the landmark Civil Service Reform Act of 1978, with its original "enterprise" vision of the federal Senior Executive Service (SES). That vision is entirely consistent with our view of enterprise leadership, but it has never really become a reality, in part because the policy and administrative infrastructure was never put in place to make it so. And as a consequence, no enterprise-wide system exists to develop leaders. To be sure, there are rules—OPM has issued many policies that guide and manage the development of government managers and leaders—but those rules do not a system make. Rather, by design or default, those rules leave leadership development almost exclusively to individual departments and agencies; as a consequence, the commitment to (and concomitant investment in) leadership development has been uneven at best. Leadership development in the federal government is a collection of largely unconnected, misaligned systems that we contend is insufficient to meet the leadership challenges a twenty-first-century government must face as an enterprise.

This is not to suggest a one-size-fits-all framework, nor is it to advocate an approach that comes at the expense of, or supplants, agency-centric leadership development efforts. Such approaches simply are not feasible given the variety of federal departments and agencies, and their continuing need for leaders steeped in their specific missions and management functions. Rather, we argue for a bold, more systematic enterprise approach to leadership development, one that is both rigorous and self-sustaining—that is, far less dependent on the interest and commitment (or lack thereof) of individual department and agency heads—so as to ensure the development of leaders of the highest quality in both good times and bad. We believe that the federal government can increase the supply of enterprise leaders by taking a more systematic, "life cycle" approach to enterprise leadership development, from the identification and development of enterprise executive candidates to their selection, evaluation, and deployment as senior leaders of the federal enterprise.

Recommendation 1: Establish Enterprise Leadership as an OPM Executive Core Qualification

Assuming a case has been made for the need for enterprise leaders, that need must be formally acknowledged to ensure that the government's leadership development "system" responds. Simply put, if the federal government wants enterprise leaders, it will have to require it. Accordingly, we recommend that the OPM establish a sixth Executive Core Qualification (ECQ) entitled "Leading the Enterprise" as a prerequisite to SES selection, equal in weight to the original (and enduring) five ECQs: Leading Change, Leading People, Results Driven, Business Acumen, and Building Coalitions. This new enterprise ECQ comprises some of the competencies chronicled in the chapters of this book, such as:

—The ability to exercise influence without formal authority and to use that influence to create a climate of trust to unify various actors and stakeholders, each with different backgrounds and interests.

—The ability to lead effectively and efficiently across organizational and institutional boundaries, leveraging common goals and shared experiences and values to achieve positive enterprise outcomes.

—A deep understanding of the structures and cultures of the particular constellation of governmental and nongovernmental organizations that must come together to tackle a particular wicked problem, and of how they interact systemically.

—The ability to build, maintain, repair, and leverage collaborative interagency networks of trusted relationships to achieve a common purpose.

We note that both the U.S. Intelligence Community (IC) and the Defense Department have validated similar ECQs and require them for certain of their senior leadership positions (in the case of the IC, it is a requirement for *all* candidates competing for a senior position), and the OPM could build upon those efforts. If the IC's experience, as recounted in chapter 10, is any guide, that "simple" mandate brings with it a whole host of administrative details that need to be resolved. In addition, given the relative shortage of enterprise-qualified senior executives (not to mention enterprise-qualified executive candidates), that requirement would have to be phased in over time. However, the payoff is evident—as illustrated in the preceding chapters, establishing a requirement will most assuredly drive enterprise leadership behavior.

Moreover, while we firmly believe that all SES members should be able to demonstrate the leadership competencies associated with a Leading the Enterprise ECQ, the fact is that much of their day-to-day leadership responsibilities will remain largely agency-centric. And while even agency-centric executives must be able to operate in an interagency environment, sometimes at a moment's notice, we also contend that there is a subset of SES (and equivalent) positions across government that have what are almost exclusively enterprise responsibilities, day in and day out—for example, an executive in one of the federal government's central management agencies. The OPM should identify and elevate that elite subset of "enterprise executive" positions, and in collaboration with the President's Management Council, manage them more centrally, as a true "corporate" resource. And they should be compensated accordingly.[2]

Recommendation 2: Require Interagency Assignments as a Prerequisite for Promotion to the SES

We also recommend that the OPM establish formal requirements for satisfying the Leading the Enterprise ECQ, to include at least one interagency developmental assignment of between one and two years. In our view, given that interagency mobility of any kind (including rotational assignments for developmental purposes) remains an "unnatural act" for most government professionals—and especially those who aspire to the SES—the only way to ensure that executives-to-be acquire an enterprise perspective and the competencies that come with it is to mandate them. As former director of national intelligence McConnell describes in chapter 2, our military (and later, our intelligence community) learned this lesson the hard way, and in both cases, it took an act of Congress to force the development of enterprise leaders through "joint duty" assignments. We believe it will take something similar to achieve the same goal for the rest of government. This mandate is already in place for military officers and civilians in the U.S. Intelligence Community (at least those who aspire to flag or senior rank). It is also entirely consistent with the tenets of Executive Order 13434, which encourages such developmental assignments for those federal employees who are designated as national security professionals, as well as with provisions in the recently passed National Defense Authorization Act for Fiscal Year 2013.

Yet the requirement to complete an interagency assignment, while necessary to the development of an enterprise leader, is not sufficient for success. The requirement must be supported (and operationalized) by administrative rules and infrastructure to make it work. This was a lesson learned first in the U.S. military's implementation of the Goldwater-Nichols Act and later in the U.S. Intelligence Community's adaptation of that concept to civilian executive development. The requisite infrastructure need not be elaborate, but we believe it must possess two essential components: first, a web-based exchange operated by the OPM where agencies and individuals could advertise, apply for, and otherwise broker rotational assignments through interagency exchange agreements and the like; and second, dedicated support staff at the agency level to help individual SES candidates find a suitable assignment and to manage the flow of those candidates out of and into the agencies. The latter function could be performed by agency Candidate Development Program or executive resources staffs, repurposed (as outlined below) to take a more strategic view of SES candidate development.

Recommendation 3: Strengthen SES Candidate Development and Make It Mandatory

We propose that the federal government's senior executive candidate development apparatus must be retooled to produce more enterprise-qualified leaders in a way that is both systematic and strategic. At present a small proportion of SES vacancies are filled by graduates of OPM-certified agency SES Candidate Development Programs (CDPs). These programs represent a special pathway because graduates of such programs can be noncompetitively promoted to the SES. On paper, the reliance on a twelve-month CDP "pipeline" to ensure an adequate supply of qualified SES candidates would seem to be effective (and significantly less time consuming) than an ad hoc, vacancy-by-vacancy approach; however, this mechanism has critical weaknesses. First, not all agencies have CDPs. Second, the track record of agencies that do have CDPs is troubling: studies have indicated consistently that far fewer than half of CDP graduates are ever promoted to the SES, a sure sign that these well-intended programs are just not achieving their desired purpose. Such a low rate implies that selection into the CDPs, their actual content, or the promotion of graduates is problematic. As a consequence, most SES vacancies are filled through what presently is a time-consuming, vacancy-by-vacancy approach that ultimately undermines the goal of strategic succession planning.

In our view, the current arrangement is not a recipe for successful executive succession. If CDPs are ever to be effective at preparing individuals for senior rank and ensuring an adequate SES succession pool, they must be significantly strengthened and more strategic, and we believe the best way to do that is to force the issue—either that or abandon them altogether. To start, we would rename (and thus refocus) them, from Candidate Development Program to Candidate Development *Process*, a rebranding designed to reflect that fact that leadership development is just that: a years-long process guided by both individual and organizational interests and requirements, not just a program that someone checks off upon completion.

To ensure that CDPs are sufficiently rigorous and, more importantly, actually produce graduates that agencies will place in SES positions, we believe the OPM should significantly raise the bar for CDP certification—actually, we prefer the term "accreditation"—establishing far more stringent *process* and content requirements. For example, CDPs should include a well thought out succession plan for key senior executive positions; formal, graduate-level leadership education, individually or in cohorts or both; managed intra- and interagency developmental assignments; and continuous assessment and feedback. These accreditation requirements would be set by the OPM, but in order to ensure senior leadership acceptance and credibility, we recommend that the OPM establish an SES Professional Development Board comprising select subcabinet officials of the President's Management Council, executive development experts from both inside and outside government, and highly regarded career senior executives (both serving and former). That board would set accreditation standards and also evaluate and approve CDPs.

We also believe that it is vital to allow private providers to apply for CDP accreditation. These providers—such as experts in succession planning or leadership assessment and coaching, academic institutions, and leadership educators—working separately or in consortiums, could offer high-quality candidate development for individual agencies and interagency candidate cohorts. Such providers would offer a viable alternative for those agencies that do not have sufficient scale or resources to establish and administer their own full-fledged CDP, and they would allow for a certain level of competition that would drive continual improvement and reduced cost, for both agencies and private providers alike. All agencies would still be required to have a Candidate Development Process, but they could outsource it (or at least much of it as parts of a CDP would likely be inherently governmental) as long as the provider was accredited.

Admission to these far more comprehensive (and intensive) CDPs could follow one of two models. An open enrollment model casts the widest possible net by allowing anyone to self-nominate and enroll, with the expectation that "up or out" evaluations each year would cut significant numbers from the CDP, based on actual development and performance. Alternatively, entry into a CDP could be competitive and selective, relying on assessment centers and other state-of-the-art tools to evaluate and select a limited number of CDP participants. There are advantages and disadvantages to each of these two models, but in either case, we believe that candidates must meet high standards to successfully complete the Candidate Development Process. Indeed, with both approaches, we believe that participants should be subject to a periodic, up-or-out evaluation against tough developmental standards. Thus agencies would be assured that those who successfully completed the CDP were indeed ready for senior executive rank.

We further believe that CDPs, as their reconstituted name implies, should have a years-long focus, identifying promising candidates early on in their careers, perhaps at General Schedule (GS) grade 12 or 13, and developing them over time—in other words, managing an agency's entire leadership and executive development pipeline. After all, enterprise leaders are not developed in a year, nor do they become world-class by accident. At the same time, we do not advocate a closed, bottom-up model that precludes admission of talented individuals at midcareer, "late bloomers" who demonstrate the aptitude and aspiration for leadership.

Above all, our version of a CDP must be flexible in that regard, finding and developing enterprise leadership talent whenever and wherever it can. That broad, integrated approach is in sharp contrast to today's relatively short-term, "finishing school" focus that limits CDP admission to GS-15 (and occasionally GS-14) candidates and delivers training in a short span of time with limited or no assessment of development. We believe this finishing school approach is one of the reasons that today's CDPs have such a poor track record, and why many have become nothing more than a consolation prize for those not selected for the SES.

Requiring more rigorous CDPs does little good if agencies can simply opt out. And even if they have an accredited, top-of-the-line

CDP, nothing today would prevent them from repeating history and ignoring its graduates. We would go so far as to make CDPs mandatory—every agency would be required to have one, with smaller agencies forming consortiums to achieve sufficient scale to establish in-house or outsourced programs.

We would go even further and argue that once this new, far more rigorous SES candidate development regime is in place and fully implemented, only those who successfully complete the process can be selected for an SES position. In some instances, it is beneficial for agencies to hire executives from outside of the government. We believe that such hires should be allowed but also limited in terms of the proportion of SES hires. Moreover, executives recruited from outside government should have to complete some portion of the process postappointment, remaining on probation until they do so. Because all new SES members are on probation for their first year anyway, this requirement would not serve as a deterrent to external or "last minute" SES appointments.

Recommendation 4: Require Formal Leadership Education as Part of Executive Development

As stated above, we believe that CDPs must include a mandatory leadership education component and that it must be provided only by those organizations that can meet rigorous government-wide CDP accreditation standards.[3] Some agencies are already leading the way. For example, the Defense Department offers its intensive APEX and Vanguard leadership development programs to SES members from the military services and its various combat support agencies, and both are designed to equip the department's civilian executives to "Lead the Defense Enterprise" (its own sixth ECQ).

APEX provides a thirty-person cohort of first-year senior executives from across the Defense Department with a comprehensive overview of that defense enterprise. It features intimate discussions with the department's most senior civilian and military leaders, including the secretary of defense and the chairman of the Joint Chiefs; exposes participants to the elements of our national security strategy and the military forces that execute it; and then takes them on an intensive "grand tour" of operational installations and joint, combatant commands, where they have an opportunity to engage directly with senior military commanders and their troops.

If APEX is an orientation to the defense enterprise, Vanguard is the grad school, focusing on leading in an interagency, enterprise environment. It too involves a cohort of senior executives, but they are more seasoned—the course requires at least five years of executive experience—and they also are more diverse, drawn not just from the Defense Department but also from other departments and agencies (for example, the Departments of Homeland Security and Veterans Affairs, or the U.S. Intelligence Community). They too have an opportunity to converse with senior leaders, but unlike APEX, Vanguard's faculty consists of leadership experts from all across government and even the private sector (including several contributors to this volume: McConnell, Allen and Marcus, Tamburrino, Sanders, and Cross) who share their perspectives and leadership lessons learned.

The IC has a similar program, in this case delivered by the University of Michigan and the Office of the Director of National Intelligence. And the President's Management Council launched its revolutionary Leading EDGE leadership development program on a government-wide basis in 2012. The program, described in greater detail by its executive director, Jim Trinka, in chapter 9, is the first one of its kind designed expressly to cultivate an enterprise identity among career federal senior executives and to help them build collaborative interagency networks. The OPM also has sponsored a series of workshops on the meta-leadership framework as well, bringing together interagency groups of senior managers and executives to learn about its approach to crosscutting crisis situations (summarized by Marcus, Allen, and Dorn in chapter 4).[4]

However, the government's overall capacity to deliver cutting edge formal education in enterprise leadership is limited. For example, while the OPM's Federal Executive Institute has developed a curriculum that is consonant with the original enterprise vision of the SES, it will never have the capacity to meet the CDP pipeline requirements we have proposed. That capacity gap can be filled by educational institutions and other providers that customize their content and delivery to government needs. For example, the Brookings Institution, through its Brookings Executive Education (known as BEE), in conjunction with the Washington University in St. Louis, offers a Master of Science in Leadership designed specifically for the Executive Core Qualifications. The program entails both coursework and the measurement and evaluation of capabilities in the field for ECQs and enterprise-related skills. Brookings Executive Education also offers certificates in leadership and policy strategy, including a course specifically designed to teach enterprise leadership to SES members and candidates. In fact, we team-teach a course entitled Enterprise Leadership.

Recommendation 5: Build the Necessary Infrastructure to Sustain the Candidate Development Process

We believe that our recommendations will serve as the foundation for a truly enterprise-focused leadership development system, one that will better leverage heretofore separate agency executive development efforts—not to replace them but rather to integrate them for the good of the greater enterprise. We also feel that the policies we have advocated—from a sixth "enterprise" ECQ and mandatory interagency developmental assignments to formal leadership education and CDP accreditation—will go far to ensure that the individuals, organizations, and the larger federal enterprise will make the investments in leadership development that are necessary to address our nation's wicked problems. However, to ensure that the system can become more-or-less self-sustaining in that regard, we believe there are some additional steps that the OPM must take.

First, so that the federal government can have insight into the state of its senior leadership corps—its strengths and gaps, its diversity and dynamics, its quality and competence—the OPM should establish and maintain an electronic registry of all SES members and their senior equivalents across government. That registry would contain detailed, up-to-date information on an individual executive's leadership career (such things as assignments and accomplishments, areas of expertise, schooling, formal evaluations, and 360-degree assessments), all in a searchable database. The registry should also include CDP graduates.

Second, the OPM should maintain a running inventory of all SES vacancies and, using the aforementioned executive registry to identify potential candidates, offer the advertising agencies slates of highly qualified candidates. The advertising agency would not be required to select from the slate (nor would executives be forced to be on it), but it would be in a position to consider the talent available from across the enterprise. We note that the OPM already posts all SES vacancies via its USA Jobs website, but that posting is ministerial, a passive administrative function. We recommend that the OPM use that information to enable a more enterprise-oriented approach to executive staffing.

Third, to enable agencies to find the very best qualified leaders (from inside *and* outside government) to fill those key leadership vacancies, the OPM should establish an "executive search" capability and make it available to them. It is well known that the most talented leaders, including those in government, are not in the market for a new job. By definition, they are highly successful just where they are and probably do not even look at SES vacancy announcements. The best have to be recruited, especially when it comes to interagency placements. This internal search-and-recruit capability would be enabled by our other recommendations—an executive registry and database of pending SES vacancies—and the OPM could provide it via its own staff, via contracts with one or more private executive search firms, or both. Agencies could access either on a fee-per-search basis.

With these mechanisms in place, the OPM would be in a position to broker (*not* force) SES mobility and developmental assignments, a prospect made far more likely with OPM's recent establishment of a common, government-wide SES performance management system, featuring uniform performance elements for all executives (see Steve Shih's description in chapter 12). As the IC experience with civilian joint duty demonstrates, disparate performance evaluation schemes are one of the principal impediments to interagency developmental assignments, so the OPM's efforts at greater uniformity at the SES level are to be commended. However, we advocate going further. As discussed in Recommendation 3 above, we believe that the OPM should also broker pre-SES developmental assignments for CDP candidates, to satisfy the Leading the Enterprise ECQ, and we would advocate a uniform performance evaluation system (patterned after the new SES one) for those candidates as well.

Closing the Leadership Talent Gap

In making these proposals, we have tried to focus on those necessary and sufficient recommendations that we believe are both bold *and* feasible. Indeed, they are based on best practices that have been previously implemented somewhere in the federal government, so in that respect, our approach is not especially revolutionary. What is revolutionary, however, is their proposed uniform application across the entire federal enterprise. That set of proposals is new, and to be successful, it will require that some aspects of federal leadership development be coordinated—and in some cases, regulated—more centrally.

Note that we are not suggesting a one-size-fits-all approach to SES development. To the contrary, while the OPM sets uniform, enterprise-wide standards for CDP quality and content (the five ECQs are an existing example), under our scheme, agencies would be given wide latitude to design programs that fit their mission, size, structure, and so on—as long as they met government-wide accreditation standards. We acknowledge that these requirements would have to be phased in over some years to provide agencies with adequate lead time to develop their programs, for the OPM to certify them, and to avoid disenfranchising individuals who have been groomed for executive succession "the old-fashioned way" on the job.

Nevertheless, we certainly expect resistance to our proposals. Under the federal government's present vertical organizational structure, no department or agency head will want to "give up" decision rights and control over his or her senior career executives or their development. Indeed, the present system creates incentives for vertical stovepiping, which is precisely what enterprise leadership is designed to overcome. Yet, even in today's agency-centric leadership environment, we know of instances, like some of those chronicled in this book, where the need to serve the greater good has won the day. We therefore are hopeful that when taken in the appropriate context, what we propose will be viewed as a possible path forward.

Here is the bottom line: while some will argue that the steps we have proposed are draconian, we contend that without them, today's substandard status quo will prevail. That is, agencies will continue to underinvest in leader development; the quality of their executive and leadership development programs will remain uneven across the federal enterprise, subject to the vagaries of budget or the personal predilections of political appointees; and perhaps most important, the quality of their leaders will continue to be questioned by those they lead.

The nation's problems are too wicked, and the need for effective government enterprise leaders too great, to allow the status quo to prevail. Indeed, the federal government reached a similar conclusion several years ago with respect to its corps of acquisition professionals and took aggressive steps to set tough standards to improve their training and education, and as a consequence, their performance. We suggest nothing less for the government's senior leadership corps.

Notes

1. Office of Personnel Management, *2012 Federal Employee Viewpoint Survey Results: Employees Influencing Change*, Governmentwide Management Report (www.fedview.opm.gov/2012files/2012_Government_Management_Report.PDF).

2. A similar effort was begun under Executive Order 13434, which required agencies to identify national security professionals and prepare them for interagency leadership positions. That effort has largely atrophied, in part because it had no consequences—a critical factor addressed in Recommendation 2.

3. We do not mean to suggest that only accredited educational institutions need apply. There should be no restrictions on who could seek CDP accreditation.

4. Sanders's firm, Booz Allen Hamilton, is on contract with the Defense Department, the President's Management Council (through Veterans Affairs), and the OPM to support those various leadership education experiences, and he leads all three engagements.

 # Contributors

Admiral Thad Allen retired as commandant of the Coast Guard in 2010 after serving as the principal federal official for the Hurricane Katrina response in 2005 and the national incident commander for the Deepwater Horizon oil spill in 2010. He is an executive vice president at Booz Allen Hamilton, a member of the Council on Foreign Relations, and a fellow at the National Academy of Public Administration. Allen holds advanced degrees from George Washington University and Massachusetts Institute of Technology Sloan School of Management.

David Altman is vice president and managing director of the Center for Creative Leadership–Europe, Middle East, Africa (CCL-EMEA). Previously, he served as CCL's vice president, senior vice president, and executive vice president of research, innovation, and product development. Earlier in his career, Altman spent ten years as a professor of public health sciences and pediatrics at Wake Forest University School of Medicine and ten years as a research scientist at the Stanford University School of Medicine. He received his master's and doctorate degrees in social ecology from the University of California, Irvine.

Donna Chrobot-Mason is an associate professor at the University of Cincinnati and also serves as the director for the university's Center for Organizational Leadership. She is an organizational psychologist with expertise in leadership across differences and in designing organizational initiatives to promote diversity and inclusion. Chrobot-Mason earned her doctorate in applied psychology from the University of Georgia. She coauthored *Boundary Spanning Leadership: Six Practices for Solving Problems, Driving Innovation, and Transforming Organizations* (McGraw-Hill, 2010). She also serves as an adjunct scholar and leadership consultant with the Center for Creative Leadership.

Rob Cross is a professor of management at the University of Virginia and research director of the Network Roundtable, a consortium of organizations sponsoring research on network applications to critical management issues. Cross has worked directly with more than 200 strategically important networks across more than 120 well-known organizations in consulting, pharmaceuticals, software, electronics and computer manufacturers, consumer products, financial services, petroleum, heavy equipment manufacturing, chemicals, and government. Ideas emerging from his research have resulted in two books, four book chapters, and twenty-three articles, several of which have won awards.

Kristin Cullen is a faculty member in research, innovation, and product development at the Center for Creative Leadership. Cullen's work focuses on leadership development, including improving leaders' understanding of organizational networks and the organizations' ability to facilitate collective leadership, complex collaboration, and change across organizational boundaries. She holds master's and doctorate degrees in industrial-organizational psychology from Auburn University.

Barry Dorn is associate director of the Program for Health Care Negotiation and Conflict Resolution at the Harvard School of Public Health. He is also clinical professor of orthopedic surgery at the Tufts University School of Medicine and held the position of interim president and CEO of Winchester Hospital, Winchester, Massachusetts. Dorn's work in preparedness dates from the events of September 11, 2001, and he has conducted research on both domestic and international leaders in order to better understand the thinking and methods that form effective crisis leadership. From this work was born the idea and practice of meta-leadership.

Andrew Hargadon holds the Charles J. Soderquist chair in entrepreneurship and is professor of technology management at the Graduate School of Management at University of California, Davis. Hargadon's research focuses on the effective management of innovation and entrepreneurship. He is author of *How Breakthroughs Happen: The Surprising Truth about How Companies Innovate* (Harvard Business School Press, 2003) as well as numerous articles and chapters in leading scholarly and applied publications.

Leonard Marcus is founding codirector of the National Preparedness Leadership Initiative, a joint program of Harvard School of Public Health (HSPH) and Harvard's Kennedy School of Government. Marcus' research, teaching, and consultation have played a key role in national and international counterterrorism efforts and in emergency preparedness and response. He has pioneered development of the conceptual and pragmatic basis for meta-Leadership. Marcus also is founding director of the Program for Health Care Negotiation and Conflict Resolution at HSPH and lead author of the primary text in the field, *Renegotiating Health Care: Resolving Conflict to Build Collaboration: Second Edition* (Jossey-Bass, 2011).

J. Michael McConnell is vice chairman of Booz Allen Hamilton, where his primary roles include serving on the firm's leadership team and leading Booz Allen's rapidly expanding cyber business. McConnell joined Booz Allen after retiring from the U.S. Navy in 1996 as a vice admiral. In 2007 he left the firm to serve as the director of national intelligence and returned in 2009 to lead the firm's intelligence business. McConnell holds a master's degree in public administration from George Washington University and is a graduate of the National Defense University and the National Defense Intelligence College.

Laura Miller Craig is a senior analyst for strategic issues with the U.S. Government Accountability Office (GAO), where she manages research and audits related to performance management, interagency collaboration, federal human capital, and other issues that can make or break the federal government's ability to address twenty-first-century problems. Before serving at the GAO, Miller Craig served as deputy director for strategic planning at the Illinois Department of Employment Security, where she was responsible for strategic planning and performance reporting for the state's unemployment insurance, workforce development, and labor exchange programs. She was central to Illinois' first statewide effort to monitor key workforce and economic performance indicators, and coauthored a report on benchmarking. Miller Craig also held management positions at the City of Chicago and at the Chicago Housing Authority. She holds a master's degree in public policy from University of Chicago Harris School of Public Policy.

Jackson Nickerson is the associate dean and director of Brookings Executive Education and the Frahm Family professor of organization and strategy at Washington University in St. Louis's Olin Business School. Nickerson is the author of several books and numerous research publications. His research focuses on critical thinking, innovation, organizational choice and performance, and leadership. In addition to consulting with numerous businesses, government agencies, and nonprofits on these topics, he is on the board of NFORMD.NET, a new media educational company. Before receiving his master's in business administration and doctorate from the Haas School of Business at University of California, Berkeley, Nickerson was a control systems engineer with NASA's Jet Propulsion Laboratory. He also holds a master's of science in mechanical engineering from University of California, Berkeley, and is a graduate of Worcester Polytechnic Institute.

Jessica Nierenberg is a senior analyst for strategic issues with the U.S. Government Accountability Office. Her research focuses on improving government performance, with a recent emphasis on the federal government's cross-organizational work with key state, local, and nonprofit partners. Previously she spent a year in Venice, Italy, as a Fulbright fellow researching the local community's response to the MOSE Project, a controversial megaproject designed to protect the city during storms and subsequent flooding. Nierenberg has a master's degree in public policy from the UCLA School of Public Administration.

Salvatore Parise is an associate professor in the Technology, Operations, and Information Management Division at Babson College. His principal research focuses on how organizations are using social media platforms, both internally among employees and externally among customers and partners. His other research focuses on using social network analysis to understand innovation, talent management, technology-mediated networks, and worker performance. Parise has received several research grants from Babson College as well as from different corporate sponsors, and his work has been published in several leading academic and management journals. Before obtaining his doctorate in business at Boston University, Parise was an engineer and researcher at IBM.

Ronald Sanders is a vice president with Booz Allen Hamilton and its first fellow. Joining the firm after thirty-seven years in federal service, he had served as the U.S. Intelligence Community's chief human capital officer, the Office of Personnel Management's associate director for policy, the Internal Revenue Service's chief human resources officer, and the Defense Department's director of civilian personnel. He is the recipient of three Presidential Rank Awards, two Theodore Roosevelt Distinguished Public Service Awards from the Office of Personnel Management, the National Intelligence Distinguished Service Medal, the Defense Department's Distinguished Civilian Service Medal, and an Innovations in American Government Award from Harvard's Kennedy School of Government, among other honors. Sanders is also a fellow of the National Academy of Public Administration and has taught at and directed research centers at Syracuse University's Maxwell School and at George Washington University.

Stephen T. Shih serves at the U.S. Office of Personnel Management (OPM) in the position of deputy associate director for executive resources and employee development. In this capacity, Shih leads OPM's office responsible for managing the overall federal personnel program relating to the Senior Executive Service and other senior professionals. He is responsible for the development and implementation of regulations and policies, as well as providing day-to-day oversight and assistance to agencies, regarding the selection, development, performance management, compensation, and recognition of federal executives and senior professionals. Shih is also responsible for providing government-wide leadership to agencies for all other federal employees with respect to performance management, awards, and leadership development.

Pasquale (Pat) Tamburrino Jr. serves as the chief of staff to the under secretary of defense for personnel and readiness. His responsibilities include policy and oversight of plans, policies, and programs that affect the recruitment, career development, pay, and benefits for 1.4 million active duty military personnel, 1.3 million National Guard and reserve personnel, and 680,000 Defense Department civilian employees. He was appointed to the Senior Executive Service in February 1997 and has thirty-six years of federal service, including seven years as an active duty naval officer. Tamburrino received the Navy Civilian Meritorious Medal in 1996 and Navy Superior Service Medals in 2003 and 2005. He was awarded the Presidential Rank of Meritorious Executive in September 2001 and was recognized with the Presidential Rank of Distinguished Executive in both 2004 and 2009—one of only two navy executives to be recognized twice at this level. Tamburrino was also recognized with the Department of Defense Fifty-Second Annual Distinguished Civilian Service Award in November 2007. He holds a master's degree in business administration from Rensselaer Polytechnic Institute.

Jim Trinka is an executive director in the Department of Veterans Affairs, where he designs, develops, and delivers a government-wide executive development program called Leading EDGE (Executives Driving Excellence in Government) initiated by the President's Management Council to help busy executives face challenges of smaller budgets, growing mission demands, and increased complexity. The program facilitates collaboration and inspires a shared government-wide identity and vision among senior executives. Previously Trinka held executive leadership roles in learning and development with the Federal Aviation Administration, the

Federal Bureau of Investigation, and the Internal Revenue Service. He began his government service with a distinguished twenty-two-year career as a fighter pilot in the U.S. Air Force. Trinka holds a doctorate degree in international politics from George Washington University.

Thomas W. Valente is a professor in the Department of Preventive Medicine, Institute for Prevention Research, Keck School of Medicine, University of Southern California. He is author of *Social Networks and Health: Models, Methods, and Applications* (Oxford University Press); *Evaluating Health Promotion Programs* (Oxford University Press); *Network Models of the Diffusion of Innovations* (Hampton Press); and over 120 articles and chapters on social networks, behavior change, and program evaluation. Valente uses social network analysis, health communication, and mathematical models to implement and evaluate health promotion programs designed to prevent tobacco and substance abuse, unintended fertility, and sexually transmitted diseases and HIV infections.

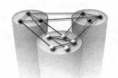

Index

ment instead of command, 9. *See
also* Interagency rotation programs; Leadership; IC Civilian
Joint Duty Program: Leading
EDGE; Networks; Wicked problems and challenges
Enterprise leadership—meta-
leadership: advantages of, 48,
54–56; characteristics of, 38, 52,
53; definition of, 37, 39; dimension 1: person and response of the
meta-leader, 42–44; dimension 2:
the situation, 45–47; dimension 3:
leading down, 47–50; dimension
4: leading up, 50–52; dimension
5: leading across, 52–54; general
dimensions and mindset of, 8,
38–42; political issues and, 45,
55–56. *See also* Disasters and
crises
Enterprise leadership—specific leaders. *See* Allen, Thad (Admiral);
Clapper, James; Dorn, Bobby;
Long, Letitia; Marcus, Leonard;
McConnell, J. Michael ("Mike");
Morell, Michael; Sanders, Ron;
Shih, Steve; Tamburrino, Pasquale
(Pat) M., Jr.; Thomas, Rick; Trinka, Jim
Enterprise leadership—strategies:
cross-agency collaboration,
13–15, 19–21, 53; designing and
managing interagency programs,
14, 36; enterprise leadership and,
39–40; everyday leading and
functioning, 54–55; innovation,
collaboration, and integration,
11, 22–23; interagency job rotation, 14; intergroup collaboration, 12; network governance, 10;
organization silos and network-
perspectives, 11, 27–28, 87. *See
also* DOD-VA Veterans Employment Initiative Task Force

Environmental Protection Agency
(EPA), 53
EOs. *See* Executive orders
EPA. *See* Environmental Protection
Agency
Executive Core Qualifications
(ECQs), 169, 171–72, 179–80,
181, 188–89, 191. *See also* Lead-
ing the Enterprise ECQ; Lead the
Defense Enterprise ECQ
Executive Office of the President, 135
Executive orders (EOs): 12333 (Rea-
gan; U.S. intelligence activities;
1981), 23–26; 13434 (Bush; na-
tional security professional devel-
opment; 2007), 181–82; 13470
(Bush; amendments to EO 12333;
2008), 27
Exxon Valdez oil spill (1989), 41

FBI. *See* Federal Bureau of Investiga-
tion
FDA. *See* Food and Drug Adminis-
tration
Federal Bureau of Investigation (FBI),
137
Federal Emergency Management
Agency (FEMA), 48
Federal Employee Viewpoint Survey
(OPM), 175
Federal Executive Institute (FEI;
OPM), 125–26, 188
Federal government. *See*
Government—federal
Federal On-Scene Coordinator, 41
FEI. *See* Federal Executive Institute
FEMA. *See* Federal Emergency Man-
agement Agency
Fish and Wildlife Service, 53
Flow Rate Technical Group, 54. *See
also* Deepwater Horizon oil spill;
Interagency Solutions Group
Food and Drug Administration
(FDA), 53

181–82; strengthen SES candidate development and make it mandatory, 182–86

Responsible party (RP). *See* Government—federal

Robert Wood Johnson Foundation (RWJF), 110–14

RP (Responsible party). *See* Government—federal

Rumsfeld, Donald, 143

RWJF. *See* Robert Wood Johnson Foundation

Sammies. *See* Service to America Medals

Sanders, Ronald, 1–15, 131–52, 174–92, 198

SBA. *See* Small Business Administration

Senior Executive Service (SES): candidate development, 172, 182–86; electronic registry of, 189; as an enterprise asset, 165–66, 173; enterprise leadership in, 14–15, 170–73, 180–81, 182; future framework and options of, 168–73; goals of, 166; history and past of, 166, 178; inventory of SES vacancies, 189; management systems of, 168–73; Office of Personnel Management and, 171–72; original vision of, vii; performance appraisal system of, 172–73; present state and operations of, 167–68; Professional Development Board and, 184. *See also* Office of Personnel Management

September 11, 2001, 25, 132. *See also* 9/11 Commission

Service to America Medals (Sammies), 121, 124, 127

SES. *See* Senior Executive Service

Shih, Stephen T., 14, 165–73, 198–99

Silver, Spencer, 69

Small Business Administration (SBA), 32

State, Department of, 122, 135, 142, 154, 161

Tamburrino, Pasquale M. ("Pat"), 7–8, 29–36, 187, 199

TAP. *See* Transition Assistance Program; DOD-VA Veterans Employment Initiative Task Force

Task Force Executive Steering Group, 35. *See also* DOD-VA Veterans Employment Initiative Task Force

Test Resource Management Center, 59

Thomas, Rick, 10–11, 59–68

Transition Assistance Program (TAP), 31, 33, 34–35. *See also* DOD-VA Veterans Employment Initiative Task Force

Transition GPS (Goals, Planning, and Success), 30–31, 33. *See also* DOD-VA Veterans Employment Initiative Task Force

Treasury, Department of, 135, 142

Trinka, Jim, 13, 119–30, 187, 199–200

United States (U.S.), 165–66, 173. See also individual agencies, departments, and offices

University of Michigan, 187

U.S. *See* United States

U.S. Agency for International Development (USAID), 161

USA Jobs (website), 189

U.S. Air Force, 59–60, 122

U.S. Armed Forces, 133

U.S. Army Command and General Staff College (CGSC), 154, 160

U.S. Army Command and General Staff College Interagency Fellowship Program, 14, 160–63